From Stress to Sanity

It's About the Way You Think

Joy L. Watson

Joy L. Watson
www.mindfitnessbooks.com

The author's intent is to offer information of a general nature to help you on your quest for emotional, physical, and psychological well-being. In the event you use any of the information in this book for yourself, the author and the publisher assume no responsibility for your actions. This publication is not intended as a substitute for the advice of a healthcare professional.

Other Books by Joy L. Watson

The Up Side Of Being Down:
Healing the Dis-Ease of Negativity with Mind Fitness

Mind Fitness:
A Guide to Elevating Mental Health

Mind Fitness Children's Book:
A Guide to Esteem and Excellence Coauthored with Caron Goode

Contents

For Samantha,
my flashlight in the present.

Foreword

CARL JUNG ONCE suggested that our top priority should be exploring our inner spaces rather than our outer spaces. The Mind Fitness Program by Joy Lehni Watson opens the door to unlimited expansion and retraining of our minds. It allows us, with ease and gentleness, to explore our inner spaces and selves and expand our love and creativity.

Mind Fitness is on the cutting edge of our own self-discovery and expansion of the creative love energy that exists in the center of each of our hearts. It brings together much information for the reader in a simplified manner so that the concepts can be easily understood. This book is about retraining the mind and explains clearly and succinctly how we can change our minds by changing our attitudes.

This program is based on the principles of Attitudinal Healing. Our true state of mind has unlimited potential and does not recognize the words "can't" and "impossible." It emphasizes love as the essence of our being and demonstrates that as we learn to become disciplined in retraining our minds, we rediscover the abundance of love that has always made up our true identity. Mind Fitness helps clarify that our true purpose here is to love and forgive and that our true identity is a spiritual one.

Most importantly, Mind Fitness uses our modern understanding of the mind and points out how our positive, active imagination can unlock the doors that once imprisoned our creative potential. There are numerous clearly explained imagery processes that can actually change how we perceive others, the world, and ourselves, producing a personal transformation.

From Stress to Sanity is for all those who want to take responsibility for their lives and let go of fear, guilt, and negative thoughts. It is a book for those who want to experience zest, passion, and compassion to live in harmony with the Loving Force that created us.

Gerald Jampolsky, M.D., Psychiatrist
Center for Attitudinal Healing
Sausalito, CA

Introduction

Mind Fitness is to the mind what physical fitness is to the body

In our not-so-sane world, most people are experiencing overwhelming challenges in balancing their work, family, and community relationships. The pressures are intense. Everyone is talking about stress, and even more, everyone is *feeling* stress. We have all said, "I must be going insane," or "My life is getting crazy," or "This is nuts!"

So many of us relatively normal, productive, and well-adjusted people are having difficulty responding energetically to the multiple demands of our daily lives. We feel like we're running hard and getting nowhere. Are we *all* going insane, bonkers, nuts—or is it getting harder to feel mentally stable in our modern world?

Have you heard of physical fitness? Welcome to Mind Fitness! This book, *From Stress to Sanity*, is about optimizing yourself: teaching yourself your optimal thinking. It offers simple learning skills to help you develop a sense of renewed personal control and mental and physical health. You move from "just coping with life" to "creating your life."

Mental health is an area of growing concern to us all. When our mental health is out of balance, it robs us—as individuals and as a society—of life and the pursuit of happiness. In our never-shut-down world, with technology and communication ever-present and demanding, we as individuals and as a culture are stressed, all too often to the breaking point. Stress is increasingly viewed as a genuine, toxic substance that contributes mightily to diseases of all kinds, constricting the fulfillment of our health and life potential.

As the Decade of the Moon in the 1960s took us outward in exploring outer space, we now voyage inward with the discovery of the brain and mind's inner spaces. While physical fitness is called self-education of the body's muscles, this deeper inner awareness is a discovery of the most intimate part of ourselves: our unique minds and spirits. As we recognize physical and mental health as inseparable, our thinking changes. Many ask, "How can we promote better physical and mental health for ourselves?" I believe you will find practical answers contained in this small guide.

The term "fitness" transcends the divisions of religion, culture, age, or sex. We all recognize that there is no single right way to keep fit. We respect joggers, jazz dancers, and cyclists equally for keeping themselves physically healthy. And like the body, fitness of the mind takes many different forms according to our individual preferences. There is no wrong way to stay physically—or mentally—strong, agile, peaceful, and flexible. So, you can relax; there is no wrong way to do your Mind Fitness.

I invite you to experiment freely with the learning tools presented in the pages ahead. Developing your health and potential goes hand in hand with expanding and clarifying your life values and purposes. You can have as much fun as you want with these ideas. It is your imagination and your mind. I have worked with this material in various forms, ranging from the intimacy of personal counseling sessions to the formality of corporate settings. The overwhelming opinion is that Mind Fitness works to produce realized personal change.

Creating a daily time for inner reflection is at the heart of stress reduction and optimal mental health. Once an individual quiets him or herself, the door to reflective thinking, intuition, and contemplation opens wide. By whatever name, mindfulness, deep wisdom, clarity, and calm are forthcoming. Some people have described the change like this:

- "Now that I am taking time each day to sit quietly, I am healthier, more relaxed, with many aspects of my life moving more smoothly."
- "I am discovering a whole new depth since I have been quieting myself each day and applying reflection actively in my life."
- "I am simply more at peace and more able to respond to the important things in my life. I feel better. I feel I have control over my thoughts and reactions now."

The sensitivities you discover within your inner life will lead to improved health, increased compassionate attitudes, and renewed purpose in actions. As you focus on your mental, emotional, and spiritual wellness, you are optimizing your thinking and may find surprising new talents and directions taking shape.

As you begin your Mind Fitness, I wish you a "bon voyage" on your journey to calm and to empowering your thinking. Please let me know how your voyage is progressing. My personal journey is moving along very happily. Sculpting is one of the unexpected changes that occurred as I began doing my Mind Fitness practice. I slowly worked sculpting into my days until it was my primary form of work and expression. I carve in marble and alabaster and then have limited edition bronze castings made from the stone, allowing me to share my work with others fully. Each sculpture expresses an energy or feeling I have discovered within myself over the past few years. I have to thank my mindful, quiet times, which I call Mind Fitness, for this new life development.

You may contact me at mindfitnessbooks.com to share your experiences with Mind Fitness and discover other available Mind Fitness books and materials. My personal site, www.joywatson.com, also contains my artwork reflecting calmness and my personal empowerment resulting from a daily mindful inner practice. I look forward to hearing from you.

Joy Lehni Watson

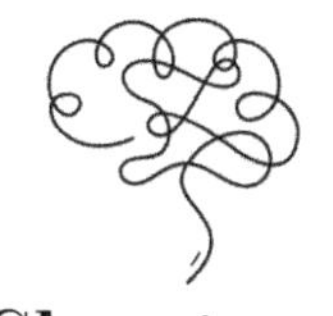

Chapter 1

Stress and Fitness

*"In three words, I can sum up everything
I've learned about life. It goes on."*
~**Robert Frost**

Out of Control

MOST PEOPLE FEEL that some portion of their life is out of control. Young or old, rich or poor, people everywhere give voice to similar complaints:

"No matter how hard I try, there isn't enough time."

"I feel so much stress."

"I just don't know how to manage it all."

"I have too many demands."

Out-of-control stress can make your attitude negative, hostile, reactionary, or just plain tired, depressed, and defeated. Life often offers few available options. Lasting satisfaction and quick solutions are fleeting experiences. In quiet moments, you may ask yourself: *How can I do it better?*

The answer lies in looking at mental fitness as we view physical fitness. Mental wellness, too, is essential to human health and well-being, particularly if the goal is to fulfill your highest potential. Doing "it" better involves turning off the noise a few minutes daily and pumping, not iron but silence coupled with ideal images.

A Mind Fitness approach to personal sanity requires a conscious shift in your thinking: from outer to inner focus, from coping to creating, from stress to balance, and from self-pity to gratitude.

If you feel trapped, with no way out, you may be feeling a bit insane at times. I use that word tongue-in-cheek to dramatize that feeling of just plain being overwhelmed—and the doubts, indecision, anger, and pessimism that result from too much stress in your life. I assure you that solutions do exist. Beyond the stress of personal entrapment lives a powerful belief in your ability—the ability to master whatever may be needed to fulfill your destiny.

You have probably experienced moments of "everything working" in the past. You can again. You can learn to do "it" better, to be calmer, and to have increased clarity of intention and sureness in direction.

Doing "It" Better

Doing "it" better in this book means you increasingly experience a balanced attainment of your goals. Doing "it" better entails becoming responsive—rather than reactive—to life situations. You become creative rather than merely coping your way through each day. You are proactive. You actively seek moments of inner calm and balance, the same way you schedule an aerobic workout. Any fitness routine, mental or physical, is a dynamic program for human change. It involves the decision not just to sit back and wait for things to happen. Instead, you pick up the reins of your life and choose to grow.

You become the executive of your mind.

This is akin to making a policy decision to empower yourself with a sense of self-determination about how you will live your life. This personal policy decision causes a shift in thinking from reactive behavior patterns of stress to internally generated modes of thought and emotion. As you expand your thinking, you can regain some control over your life.

You become proactive on your own behalf.

By paying attention to your attitudinal health:

- You empower yourself to do whatever the "it" in your life is right now.
- You plan and actively reflect on your actions with a sense of integrity.
- You create time to imagine different scenarios, sequences, and priorities.

Sanity Progression

Stress inevitably causes us to feel out of control, prompting reactions of hostility, negativity, and pessimism. We anger too quickly; we're bitter and sarcastic; life begins to look pretty grim.

Webster's Dictionary defines sanity as being "mentally healthy." I think it is safe to say that good mental health replaces that on-the-edge, pressurized feeling of freaking out with an ability to confidently respond, with varying degrees of calmness and balance, to most of life's demands. Good mental health can be viewed as a progression as we move from feeling stressed out and overwhelmed to barely, then to mostly coping and managing to get by, to finally moving towards real increases in our emotional stability and satisfaction levels. This is the balance of Basic Sanity. You are beginning to create your own life. Fuller mental health then progresses on to growing feelings of confidence to guide and empower your own life, attitudes, and behaviors…most of the time.

This feeling of Empowered Personal Sanity is a notch above plain old keeping it together. You are fulfilling your potential. You are dynamically calm. You are at peace, and yet you're stretching. You are living more often than not with an attitude of personal confidence, optimism, and a sense of dynamic love. You are genuinely happy! You feel sharp and on top of things.

Dynamic love is an ideal. It represents an attitude of optimism, a way of thinking that is positive, fluid, and enlivening to yourself and others. It is love in action, upbeat, risk-taking, and confident. Dynamic love is an attitude and energy aimed toward your life purposes. You live with a spirit of compassion and joy toward others and yourself. You experience a new openness to life. This attitude of optimism and self-direction replaces many of the old fears.

But let's start at the beginning. The natural evolution of a Mind Fitness program helps you move from overwhelming stress to stabilizing your essential mental health and attitude. You begin to quiet. Soon after you start doing a Mind Fitness practice, you feel calmer and more self-directed. You cope better with life. Basic sanity is restored. Your priorities grow more precise, and your intentions more focused. You no longer freak out unexpectedly over small things. You feel a sense of developing control in your life. You notice you have gained some distance from too many stressed-filled moments.

An Awareness Exercise

Now, think for a moment about gradually making mental fitness and mindful, proactive reflection a part of your everyday lifestyle, just as you may now make physical fitness and a nutritious diet a part of your daily life.

If bringing out the best in yourself and becoming your ideal self appeals to you, please permit yourself to include regular mind care in your life.

Let this be your starting moment.

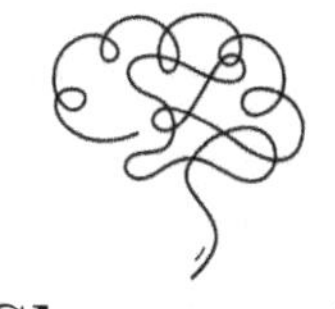

Chapter 2

Your Ideal Self

"Wisdom tells me I am nothing. Love tells me I am everything.
Between the two, my life flows."
~**Nisargadatta Maharaj**

THIS BOOK IS not about wishing on a star or covering up life's difficulties and shadows with platitudes. It's about accepting all our complexities and offering ourselves constructive methods for empowering a sense of peace, balance, and spiritual growth. These are mental tools to be used at different times. The challenge is to gain a healthy perspective on your attitudes and actions and to apply that perspective in a meaningful and ongoing way. The power lies in becoming proactively involved in your mental well-being rather than feeling buffeted by life's forces. The key to all this is *learning* to be aware and mindful.

As you put your mind and attitude into training,
you move from merely coping to creating
attitudes and goals you ideally want.

It's important to identify how you are functioning now and how you ideally want to experience your life. You do this by relaxing, quieting yourself mentally, and gaining insight into your life's purpose and direction. Learning to think reflectively using whole-brain, deep-centered thinking skills optimizes your learning, health, and performance levels— no matter who or where you are.

*People are happier and function better
as they engage in personal inner nourishment.*

Story: I first learned how to use what I now call mental fitness techniques at an early age—though I didn't know what to call them then. I often had trouble falling asleep at night. I would lie there for hours with my mind going in and out of control. One night, when I was about eight years old, my dad came in, sat on the edge of the bed, and said, "I want to tell you a little story. I want you to paint this story in your mind so that you can see it." And then, he taught me how to focus my mind by counting sheep.

"See yourself in the center of a very green meadow on a warm summer day. Can you imagine a fence with many fluffy white sheep on one side? Can you feel the warm sunshine on your face and arms?"

I said, "Yes."

"Now, I want you to imagine one of the sheep jumping over the fence to the other side. Can you see that one sheep jumping and say one in your mind? Now see the second sheep jumping and say two in your mind…."

The following day, I was trying to remember how many sheep I had counted. I only knew that I had finally fallen asleep.

This was my first experience at consciously creating images in my mind to achieve a desired end. It taught me that I could do something to quiet my anxiety and help me control my fears more. I could teach myself how to relax.

*I began to know deeply that my mind and body
were invisibly interconnected and that I had a say in
how both functioned.*

Training Your Mind

In the practice of mental fitness, what works is to structure reflective time into your life, allowing you to learn how to relax, clarify your life intentions, and activate that direction with momentum. The fitness model incorporates staying mentally and physically fit and healthy. Physical fitness is nothing new to millions who already understand how regular exercise can be central to their well-being. If you already have a physical fitness routine, now you are simply targeting emotional and mental wellness in addition to your muscle and cardiovascular strength.

You are putting your mind into training.

Taking personal responsibility for your mental stability won't cure all your stresses overnight. It demands focus and training. But it is doable. It is learnable. Many people say that their days are filled with dissatisfying tasks and that it is never enough, no matter how much they accomplish. As people begin to follow a focused personal program, they experience an immediate change. They gain a broader perspective and can reorient themselves, focusing on their essential goals. One man reported, "I immediately began to feel more in control of my thoughts. I can better sort out what's important and what's not and feel less pressured. I even feel creative occasionally." He was describing a renewed sense of empowerment.

Ask yourself:
- What do I do now to stay healthy in my body and attitude?
- What do I do now to handle life's inevitable stress?
- What do I do now to move toward my dreams and into my life goals?

After you gain a sense of how you handle things at present, ask yourself how you would like this to be different:
- How would I like myself to handle life's inevitable stress?
- How would I like to stay healthy in my body and attitude?
- How would I like to move toward my dreams and goals?

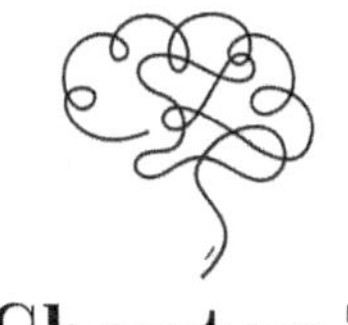

Chapter 3

What's Empowerment?

*"Each day I move toward that which I do not understand.
The result is a continuous accidental learning which
constantly shapes my life."*
~Yo-Yo Ma

Empowerment is so essential to feeling less stress and more sanity. At its best, empowerment means fulfilling your potential through being vigorously charged by life's possibilities. At the least, it means moving away from anger, victimized thinking, and blaming. Empowerment encompasses taking positive action, respecting your internal process, and actualizing your unique life path. It is an inner mental attitude matched by outward acts. When empowered, you increasingly take thoughtful risks and responsibility for yourself and how you respond.

Empowered individuals actively cultivate their abilities and character. They aim their life toward a sense of purpose that brings them happiness. To do so, they purposely focus on developing creative and critical thinking skills. They train themselves to see options where others see limitations. They encourage within themselves such purposeful thinking skills as:

- imagining the possibilities
- generating multiple options
- making their own decisions
- creatively solving "how to" and "what's next?" questions.

Empowered people think and act differently because they have trained their minds differently. In essence, the underlying mental skills lie in not only *what* they think but *how* they think.

Empowered thinking is composed of:
1. Belief: the firm belief that your goals are possible
2. Will: the will and discipline to persevere through difficult times
3. Skills: the mental, emotional, and physical skills to perform the tasks necessary to generate the quality of life you want

Empowerment is proactive—working mentally and physically to actualize your goals and dreams.

Ten Characteristics of Empowered People

- Willingness to push the comfort zone.
- Willingness to take action on your own behalf.
- A sense of your abilities and energy.
- A capacity to love quickly and easily.
- An ability to think of options and solutions.
- An ability to laugh.
- An ability to trust yourself and others.
- A willingness to trust in your intuitive intelligence.
- An openness to life's adventures.
- A tendency for work and play to overlap.

From the above list, identify empowered characteristics that you feel you are comfortable with and have within you most of the time now.

Identify a couple of the empowered characteristics you would like to increase within yourself.

Sense of Purpose

Most of us feel healthier, higher performing, and emotionally happier when we live life with a sense of purpose. Whether we are solving problems, forming new relationships, or developing new directions, having a purpose gives meaning to what we do. A sense of empowerment flows into us whenever we realize that we have chosen our life goals and know we alone are responsible for actualizing those goals. We may be amazed to discover a stronger, more compassionate, seemingly more intelligent person developing within ourselves.

We discover our power and potential for wondrous things as we balance our behaviors with our inner thoughts, actions, and attitudes. We learn to live with increasing integrity that balances and reorders our values and priorities. We are actively optimizing ourselves. As always, this is easier said than done. It requires expanding our old thinking patterns, seeing possibilities, and taking personal risks.

Pam's Story
"I finally mustered the faith to believe in myself and then the will to act on that belief."

Pam is an excellent example of making one's own life choices. She had wanted the position of personnel director in her company. Pam knew the odds were against her because she lacked formal training but wanted to try. She put herself and her attitude into active self-empowerment training. Employing her focused mind, Pam imagined herself sitting behind a desk, interviewing people. She purposefully worked to build up her self-confidence and verbal skill level. She visualized and mentally rehearsed her ability to project her wants and desires clearly and powerfully. Pam even used a mirror and a tape recorder.

When the day came for the interview, she deeply felt her power phrase: "I can do this; I know I can." She heard it over and over in her mind, and she chased away any doubts with that affirmation.

A week later, she received a phone call that the job was hers. She was ecstatic. That night, she danced around the kitchen, singing, "I am a hero in my own life. I did it; I did it!" This is a beautiful description of self-determination. Pam's potential expanded!

The high self-esteem of being a hero/heroine in your own life comes from following the path of your inner integrity, a path made up of the challenges and rewards you encounter while remaining true to yourself. You are then empowering your full potential. Your situation may or may not change, but you will have given yourself a clear attitude and direction. When you are committed to your values by bringing out the best in yourself, facing challenges with such an assertive attitude allows you to be in touch with who you are beyond all your life struggles.

You are focusing on your sense of value
and the quality of your attitude toward life.

I am reminded of a Russian woman who lived in New York for several years. Her biggest thrill about living in this country was her expanded attitude.

"I do things I could barely imagine before, such as running. I now run ten miles. When I first came, even two miles was hard to think about. Living here, I have expanded my thinking about what I can and cannot do."

Ancient Spirit

Empowered and healthy individuals learn to develop specific behaviors and personal characteristics. As people begin to train themselves toward a sense of inner quiet mentally, most experience themselves naturally learning to trust what can be called a more profound spiritual nature. This is a natural progression as they learn to follow their gut instincts.

Quiet thinking and reflection allow life experiences to be lived on many different levels. This expanded dimension of the human experience cultivates feelings of interrelatedness as larger patterns are perceived. It touches our Divine natures with a sense of mysterious wonder. Each person's different mix of these levels of awareness is a unique soul language.

That is not to say these ideas are new. Nearly all ancient cultures knew the importance and power of deep-centered techniques. We now call it mindfulness. Similar methods can be found throughout the world. Visual thinking or mental imagery is a skill that the Tibetans and Hawaiians have used for centuries. Buddhism teaches its followers to visualize the still point within all life's activities. The Jewish tradition honors the prayerful chanting of ideal directions to live one's life. Christian prayer is a form of active visual thinking combined with affirming the power of the Christ Spirit. Prayer involves articulating a higher power's grace as we seek guidance for our daily actions.

People are drawing on these ancient beliefs and knowledge systems throughout the world. We are beginning to unify diverse philosophies and native teachings more fully as we discover the benefits to health and well-being that lie within them.

Hawaiian Story

While living with my family in Hawaii for many years, I worked with a wonderful old Hawaiian woman who taught Head Start and had raised thirteen children. She used her brand of mental training to achieve many of her goals in life. Annie Haleakala had calm confidence, a sense of magic, and warm personal relationships. She lived to her potential. She would laughingly say that her key to happiness and success was "just sitting around and playing mind pictures from the best part of me. It's an old Hawaiian tradition like planting good seeds and letting them sprout."

I slowly realized that she was using a straightforward but elegant reflection method to take her where she wanted to go, at least mentally. Her mental exercise routine was to continually sow the seeds of positive thought throughout her life. Annie Haleakala was a long-distance runner of Hawaiian Mind Fitness. Her life displayed the marvelous results of her discipline, and just being in her presence was a gift.

It would be wonderful to put things on automatic pilot and have life run smoothly, but it only sometimes works that way. Painful things do happen to the nicest people, and we cannot always depend on things going smoothly in the external world. Once we understand the pivotal lesson that our lives and reactions are our responsibility, then it is only reasonable to train ourselves to maximize the journey.

This book proposes that people need regular time for proactive reflection—to pause to quiet their minds, balance their emotions, and open up to their intuitive abilities to remain mentally healthy and fulfill their potential.

Mind Fitness Exercise to Quiet Stress

You can do this exercise in the car or at your desk. It takes thirty seconds to two minutes. Read it to get a general idea, and then try mentally moving through your body, consciously relaxing each part.

I draw in three deep breaths as I feel my muscles relax.

In my mind's eye, I see my body growing loose and limp as the tensions fade. I see and feel a warmth start at the top of my head and slowly work its way down my body, releasing tension as it moves.

First, my eye muscles relax, then my cheeks, tongue, and the corners of my mouth as the warmth moves down my face.

It then moves down my neck, shoulders, and arms, carrying the stresses and tensions in its path as I see them drain out of my fingers like water from a faucet.

The warmth continues moving down my chest, back, and abdominal area, down my legs, knees, and calves.

The tensions drain away into the earth through the soles of my feet.

I draw one more deep breath, allowing all the stress to leave my body and mind. Slowly, I open my eyes.

Chapter 4

Commitment to Change— The Cycle of Personal Growth

We delight in the beauty of the butterfly, but rarely admit the
changes it has gone through to achieve that beauty.
~ Maya Angelou

Most of us slowly work to a point when we are ready to make a sustained, focused effort to change something about ourselves. And finally, with a new energy level behind that often-felt vague desire, we are ready. We want to change how we handle things to do "it" better, whatever that identified "it" is in our life. We want to commit to acting on our behalf to grow happier and more fulfilled. We are suddenly ready to enter the training of our mind and heart, using a learning approach calling for inner quieting and proactive reflection. But what can you expect as you develop a regular Mind Fitness program for yourself?

Healing Cycle for Personal Development

Personal development can, and undoubtedly will, take you into uncharted waters. Being proactive—acting on your own behalf—means pushing yourself out of your comfort zone and voting for yourself by changing unwanted habits and character patterns. It means not waiting for the world to take you there. Active identification, acceptance, and healing make up the cycle of creating your life attitudes and actions:

- **Identify** ways in which you would like to grow and develop.
- **Accept**, even embrace, growth and change as a natural result of lifelong learning.
- **Heal** by actively choosing to expand with new ways of thinking.

Reflect on the various stresses you have during the day: money, relationships, work, food, housing… If you say "everything," start to name exact times, places, and situations.

Identify which specific situations induce stress, leaving you feeling frustrated and powerless.

- What do you feel is "insane" in your life?
- What is explicitly stressing you out?
- What times of day do you experience your stress?

1. Identify ways in which you would like to grow and develop.

You will want to be very specific about what you want to develop. Start asking yourself questions in the name of your healing and happiness.

- Do I want to become a more balanced and calmer person?
- Is my lifestyle good for me?
- How would I like to act or talk in particular situations?
- What should I be paying attention to now?

Then, add more in-depth questions.

- In what ways would I like to expand my beliefs and grow?
- What is making me happy, and what is not?
- Where do I respond rather than react in my life? And where do I react instead of respond?
- How can I contribute more moments of aware peace to my stress-filled days?

- Are there changes I could make to feel less rushed or overwhelmed?

You can work on personal attributes or character issues by challenging that impatient, testy attitude that frequently pops up. You can set your goal to step back from that need to be overly controlling or to achieve perfection. In the long view of things, does it matter if everything is done in your way and timing?

Consider bringing more balance to your emotional life, such as being gentler, more assertive, or defusing a quick temper. Perhaps you are more concerned with your job and corporate life, or want to be more artistic, or direct yourself toward self-care in the physical health department. I have a friend training to walk a marathon for a charity; it's her way of expanding her limited and fearful thinking pattern of "I can't walk that far." What do you want to develop within yourself? Reflect on these questions of deep self-direction.

Patterns of impossibilities and limitations show up differently in each of us.

Whether we work as a top government official, business executive, dot-comer, teacher, operator, food server, transport or postal worker, or religious leader, we are all limited by our early thinking styles. You will want to do your soul-searching to pinpoint precisely how your way of thinking is setting limitations in your life. The clearer you get, the easier it will be to leave old patterns behind.

What are the target areas for you to change? And what precisely do you feel is holding you back? Put these thoughts in words for yourself. What old patterns are not serving you any longer? As you start to record in a journal for yourself or share some of these more intimate personal truths with another person, you begin healing and growth.

When you can, push yourself to put your thoughts into symbols, spoken and written. Do that even when it causes you to push a little past your comfort zone. The power of visual images and language cannot be overemphasized. Use visual thinking and draw a symbol or picture of what you have identified as your dead-end or sabotaging thought. Any pencil marking will do—even just a big dot. Create another image representing how you want to expand your beliefs and actions. It can be as simple as an arrow, circle, or smiling face. Any squiggle will help make your directional change more concrete. You are impressing your mind with this new direction. Try incorporating these new tools to teach yourself something new.

Be Specific

Ask yourself these personal questions, and make your answers as clear and specific as possible. You are identifying something important, so go into detail. Be specific about your private areas of change. Avoid the tendency to generalize by saying, "I want to change—well, you know, the way I talk to my kids." Get specific about the tonal quality, body language, volume, and word choice. Think it through yourself to see what you want in that change.

- What are my specific targets for change or healing?
- What is making me unhappy? What can I live with?
- What is holding me back? What personality traits are not empowering me?
- What do I need to *stop* doing to become happier?
- What do I need to *start* doing to become happier?

Much of our fearful thinking and self-sabotage is hidden from view. It takes ongoing self-awareness to recognize behaviors limiting our fulfillment and life performance. Examples may include jumping to conclusions too quickly, not listening enough to understand the larger picture, interrupting others, and giving so many details that we confuse people. We often have difficulty recognizing these behaviors in ourselves.

One woman said, "It has taken me a while to begin to see and name some long-held personal characteristics that were not benefiting me, like impatience and my overly controlling personality. When I took the time to look deeply, I realized that I was taking things too personally. I now understand that I was often focused on other people's shortcomings or looking for what they could do for me. I am learning to change my thinking and not jump all over people so quickly with *my* demands. I think I am finally taking responsibility and control in a healthier way. It has helped my relationship with my husband and family."

You may not have talked much about these things with your family or friends. In our competitive culture, people rarely acknowledge personal difficulties and self-imposed limitations. Who likes to talk about their bad attitudes? We all have hidden these subtle—and not-so-subtle—behaviors and feelings, even from ourselves. This is where support groups can be helpful. They create a safe environment for honest personal exploration. We learn from others as they express their trials and successes. Often, we see ourselves through others' experiences.

> ***Empowered change comes with increased***
> ***awareness and mindful, proactive reflection.***
> ***It is a part of our natural mental health evolution.***

You begin the growth process by recognizing and acknowledging that you carry some outgrown beliefs and are now ready to expand in positive ways. You are prepared to develop your thinking. Bob said, "I'm now growing to be more open and willing to see things differently. I have discovered a lot more options."

2. Accept, even embrace, growth and change as a natural result of lifelong learning.

Welcome trouble! We may not run out to grab it, but when it comes, we can focus on coping with it in the best way we can. We all have heard the saying: "Crisis is an opportunity for change." We all know moments and times of personal crisis. Some are life-altering—significant challenges that last for months or years; others may be as small as the impulse to irrationally explode at the salesperson you judge to be incompetent and unbearably slow. Each is a time of crisis. In your mind training work, you boldly aim to handle each crisis—big or small, lasting or fleeting—in the best, most aware way you can. Each moment is a decision on how you will react or respond. Your goal is to stay sane, even when insanity and extreme stress show up in your life.

It is much harder to change your life at certain times than others. There are times when you may be just hanging on. Just barely coping beats not coping. None of us can always control how our lives twist and turn or what lands at our feet—there are occasionally unexpected and unexplained "wild cards," as my friend Dr. Jack calls them—but it helps to remember that we have choices about how we respond to the sense of being overwhelmed and what feels like the insanity of it all. Coping and getting through those difficult times is about the best you can ask of yourself. Such times challenge us not to be defeated by them but to find renewed meaning for personal growth. The journey is to grow toward more profound compassion for yourself and others. You do that by expanding your thinking and understanding of the heart and mind.

It is so helpful to know that you can *choose* to expand your thinking, get creative, and develop a deeper understanding and personal abilities. There is nothing shameful in deciding that you want to change and grow and want a new way of handling your life. You may be ready to trade in some of your earlier beliefs and perceptions for more expansive and healthier ways of thinking. Remember that all beliefs served a purpose at one time in your life; now may be a great time to challenge those thoughts and behaviors.

By just recognizing the self-sabotaging attitudes and behaviors that are causing you pain, you empower yourself to choose to move on. The first big step is directing yourself to *trust*—that you will discover options for creating new ways to live a more fully functioning life. You may not know all the answers right now, but the answers will come as you focus on doing your best to stay balanced, calm, and sane.

Welcome playing a directing role in challenging the old and learning the new. Receive challenges and trouble as your doorway to more expansive beliefs and behaviors. You'll find this easier to do as you accept who you are, with every aspect of your personality—the ones you like and ones you don't. Look at and listen within yourself, taking on the challenge of an honest personal evaluation.

Ask yourself these questions:
- How would I describe my personality in three sentences?
- What do I like about myself?
- What would I like to change about myself?
- What do I believe is true about myself?
- What attitudes and behaviors are serving me well?
- What attitudes and behaviors are no longer serving me?
- What do I value and want to develop within my character?

It's ultimately comforting to know that we created and learned our present attitudes and mental beliefs; therefore, we can create new ones. We can keep some and evolve others. We can keep our passion for some things and focus on letting go of perfectionism or tempers. We can keep our sweet nature and let go of having to please everyone. We can keep our generous hearts and still set boundaries for our giving.

Just because something was true about you years back does not mean it has to be part of your behavior and attitudes today. Once you have identified and accepted your personal limitation patterns, you can redirect them into more satisfying and successful ways of thinking.

3. Heal by actively choosing to expand into new ways of thinking.

You have identified your specific areas for focused growth and accepted that change is not something to be ashamed of or avoided but is a natural part of our lifelong learning process. Learning to do "it" better goes on until you draw your last breath; what changes are you focusing on?

How, then, do you change and heal the self-limiting behavior patterns that no longer serve you? Try pausing, slowing down each day, actively pursuing personal peace and healing. Engaging in a Mind Fitness time of reflection and quiet teaches you how to stop, look, and listen. You learn through proactive reflection to become aware of your inner intuitive sense and visualize the kind of person you want to be. You know to give yourself more positive, supporting directions—the mental and verbal directions you need to wake up and stay aware of your choices and behaviors, moment to moment. You focus on what you want to develop in your life personally. Remember that you can only change yourself—your focus must be on responsibility to yourself and then to others.

***Healing happens when you learn to consciously
fill your mind and spirit with the elements
that make up the person you want to be.***

You heal by focusing on your internal dialogue, your "mental chatter." Notice that this can be either self-affirming or destructive, blaming or solution oriented. Focus on using empowering self-talk and thinking as often as possible. Create a steady stream of realistically optimistic, self-forgiving internal messages. Work on stopping negative, blaming, or derogatory words as you become aware.

Start becoming actively aware of the words you choose to say to yourself in your head.

- How judgmental are they?
- Do you hear yourself whining often about things you want different?
- Do you blame others when things do not go right?
- Do you hear yourself using angry, resentful words?

OR

- Is your internal chatter more often forgiving and gentle on yourself and others?
- Do you hear yourself thinking of solutions to problems?
- Do you offer yourself different possible options for actions you might take?
- Do you use words of acknowledgment and gratitude frequently?

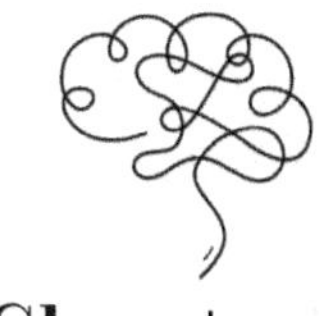

Chapter 5

Active Acknowledgment

"Catch 'em being good."

Most people have days in which they engage in negative mental chatter. It's pessimistic, it's depressing, it's cutting, it's degrading; it's full of what's known as *dissing*. How empowered and peaceful can you be if you constantly engage in negative mental chatter like this?

- "I shouldn't have done that."
- "I was too pushy back there."
- "They should feel guilty for not being on time." *Or* "I feel so guilty!"
- "Can't they do anything right?" *Or* "I can't do anything right."
- "What a lazy person! You didn't even exercise today."
- "I am sooo stressed out. I am always feeling stressed."
- "The kids are driving me crazy."
- "I am going nuts!"

On and on it can go. This negative mental chatter is the first "line of defense" that has to go when you begin creating greater inner peace and health in your life. Reduce the negativity and reframe the content of your ongoing stream of mental chatter, and you will be well on your way to feeling more in control and even a bit more sane.

It's time for a personally commanded "about-face."

An about-face means a 180-degree turnaround. Take a healing step by consciously and actively acknowledging what is going right. Most of us use internal dialogue to blame and criticize ourselves and others far more than we use it for affirmation and positive visualizations. Focus on changing directions.

Active acknowledgment can reverse the negative mental chatter you may be drowning in. It is the old "Catch 'em being good" method of positive reinforcement. Take the time to actively affirm moments when things are going well for you. Acknowledge yourself each time you become aware you're on target. This means telling yourself:

- "That was great. I was more patient than I normally would have been."
- "I did that well. I was more outgoing than usual."
- "I stood up for myself and did not let anyone run over me."
- "I was a good listener at that meeting. I didn't interrupt with my passionate responses but waited until the right time to speak."
- "I was less defensive and more open and in personal control. I conducted myself well back there."

You are learning to see with optimism and creative possibility.
If you want to be more patient, focus on deliberately developing that attribute within your personality. If you want to be more physically active, visualize and affirm that you can be more active, then go out and move your body. If you want to be a better learner, see yourself learning and affirm that you can master the material ahead, then give it some honest effort.

Get Specific and Start Noticing

I want to emphasize how important it is to be specific in your thinking and to start noticing your successes. You are now clearly moving to a new level of self-directed thinking. As you train yourself to focus on specific images and words that empower and support you, you also shy away from automatically focusing on the downside of things. Now, you are visualizing and affirming your strengths.

At first, you may need to push yourself to think of something positive, as a parent would a reluctant child. Through practice, you become aware that you have some positive personal qualities and moments, even on the most challenging days. Not that you overlook all difficulties—but you notice and acknowledge those moments in your day when you experience a flash of the Up Side. You start to build upon them, training your mind to perceive increasing fulfillment in daily life: a smile you give to someone, that moment when you let someone merge ahead of you while driving, that moment you appreciate the warm sun on your shoulder. You notice and affirm each moment of good fortune when it happens: just catching the subway or bus before it takes off, turning your head just in time to brake for a car that cuts in front of you, putting on a jacket and finding a forgotten five-dollar bill in the pocket.

Start noticing small things—this leads to a profound change.

What to Expect

You can expect a growing inner sense of confidence and calm as your perceptions expand. You are tapping into a more profound and wise part of yourself. Such shifts in thinking affect your business, work, home, and relationships. It's an ongoing process as you begin to claim your thinking content, offering guidance to your chatterbox mind about what it might want to ponder rather than allowing it to run wild.

Don't pressure yourself with the expectation that you'll consistently achieve this optimistic clarity. Instead, why not take heart that your new way of thinking is growing within you, like a seed sprouting? It will continue to germinate as long as you focus on developing the best potential in yourself and others. Slowly, surely, you *will* grow and change as you center yourself and then allow yourself to visualize and affirm that change. Mind training is lifelong, like eating, breathing, and exercising.

Attitudes = Sustained Action

The shift from intellectually understanding something and actually *doing* it is a monumental step.

It takes real self-love to begin to care deeply for yourself.

How many of us know things we should do for ourselves that we do not do? I am frequently aware of the gap between my intentions and actions. It's one thing to know you should do something as simple as flossing your teeth or taking your vitamins—doing it is a different matter. It is with sustained action that you integrate new learning and attitudes into your life.

Thinking and preparing are both good; the mind is a great friend when focused and used with clear intention. It builds a bridge, a pathway to translate inner feelings and intentions into *action*. But the mind can only go so far. *We* must cross over that bridge.

It is the sustained action that completes the learning.
Learning to think proactively comes from applying these self-development principles in your life. The centuries-old book the *I Ching* repeatedly says, "Perseverance furthers."

This is not a promise that unwanted patterns will never surface again but rather a commitment to work with them as they do.

Make the Commitment to Yourself

Making this commitment to yourself is an act of surrender through which, ironically, you gain more control over your life than previously known. Toni shared that she was "driven by fear, trying to be this powerful independent woman who thought she had the power to make it all happen herself. I was going crazy trying to create something to prove I was someone to myself and others. I had tremendous self-imposed stress. Of course, I didn't see it that way at the time. Everything was a deadline in my life."

Things fell apart on me bad. I had to surrender to a bigger vision. I had to ask for help from family and friends. Now, I am much humbler and more in touch with my interconnections and spirituality. I had to fall before growth and changes were possible. I was forced to surrender to the fact that I was not Superwoman after all—to get some perspective in my life and trust in my abilities."

***You begin to vote for yourself in the healthiest
and the most balanced way possible.***

It takes great courage to commit to real action and decide you deserve to give yourself the fullest life possible with the most possibilities. Usually, that means backing off somewhat from the high-stress, insane demands you are experiencing.

An Expansion Thinking Exercise

1. To become aware of ways in which you are limiting yourself, choose one or two areas of your thinking and belief structure that you would like to expand. It may be a belief that you cannot play music, jog a certain distance, get along well with a family member, overcome an unwanted habit pattern or personality trait, work compatibly with a coworker, or handle all the many tasks of daily living. Write down these specific areas of the desired change. For example:

   - "I want to change my relationships with coworkers/family members to become supportive and creative."
   - "I want to change my thinking that I cannot do (you name it) so I can do it."
   - "I want to change my thinking from I cannot overcome this habit to I can overcome it."

2. Know that change is a natural part of the evolutionary force. Begin to describe your willingness to grow and develop new ways of perceiving situations around you. Be specific. For example:

   - "I am willing to change my attitude in my relationship with my coworker to be more supportive and creative."
   - "I want to change my fear of not being able to stop smoking to be sure that I can stop smoking."

Remind yourself that you are choosing to proactively expand to new ways of thinking. Now is the time for action, the action of relaxation! Now is the time to start your program. You know your goals. Declare your willingness to expand, even if it takes you out of your comfort zone.

Close your eyes and take a deep breath, relaxing your body and mind. To anchor your decision, you can draw an image or symbol and affirm your decision in words. Quietly say to yourself:

- "I am now ready to commit to action. I am now ready to begin a regular personal reflection time."
- "I will spend three to five minutes in the morning reflecting, visualizing, and clarifying the day's intent."
- "I will spend five to ten minutes in the evening quietly reflecting on how I handled stress during the day."

You are on your way.

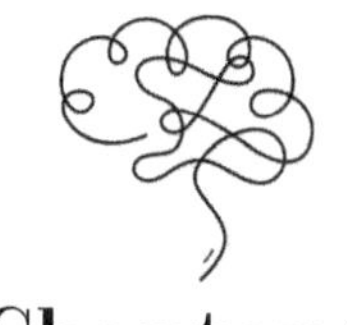

Chapter 6

Three Basic Forms of Mind Fitness

"*If I had my life to live over again, I'd be a plumber.*"
~Albert Einstein

THIS IS THE chapter of "threes"—watch for them!

1.   A quick mind lift for a flash reminder of intention and direction
2.   A short, few-minute Mind Fitness booster
3.   A full 20-minute Mind Fitness workout

Your inner training program can be accomplished through a simple routine of one to twenty minutes. This chapter describes a quick Mind Fitness booster; you'll find a longer session in Chapter Twenty-Two. Mind lifts are discussed throughout the book, especially in Chapter Thirteen.

Please remember that just a few minutes of quiet mind and body focus can greatly rebalance you. Twenty minutes is a good time zone to work up to, but for heaven's sake, you don't want to feel guilty that you are "only" doing two, five, or ten minutes! The message is to actively pause to support your mental health and development in your life. Do that the best way you can, given your time constraints.

It's ideal to do your session every day at the same time in the same place. That's why they have monasteries. Out here in the busy world, we need to make some adjustments. Personalize your program, tailoring it to fit your rhythms and life goals. Remember that these ideas are a foundation to get you started. In creating your own life, nothing is written in stone. As with physical fitness, everyone's inner workout is different. Experiment with various techniques, be creative, and ensure your routine is empowering, peaceful, and expansive.

***Reclaim control over your life by consciously
directing your body, mind, and spirit.***

After you become more accomplished with Mind Fitness, you will more easily center yourself anytime and anywhere by taking a few deep, quiet breaths. But in the beginning, the most important thing is to begin. Breathe with awareness.

Prep with Three Quick "Check-ins"

1. Simple stretching, relieving tensions

When you relax the body, you relax the mind. Stretching is one of the best ways to release tension; it also brings oxygen into your body. Take a minute or two to stretch your body and release any tightness in your joints or muscles. The mind and the body work together.

2. Preparing yourself and your posture

Make yourself comfortable enough to go within rather than staying focused on your outside physical surroundings and daily thoughts. Your preparation may be as simple as sitting in a comfortable chair, with an erect posture and feet on the floor, and closing your eyes.

3. Mentally open

Be mentally open to the unknown. Move past any resistance to new possibilities you may feel just because they are still fresh and unknown. As you relax, you use your internal dialogue to remind yourself to be open to an expansive, more comprehensive thinking style. Put away doubts and resistance for a moment; let yourself open to new possibilities, even if they do not make sense right now.

The Three Major Steps in a Mind Fitness Session

1. Focused relaxation: releasing tension and anxiety, unifying mind and body.

2. Visual thinking: giving yourself a road map for ideal outcomes with action steps.

3. Affirming: articulating your vision of success through directed word power.

Step 1: Focused relaxation—unifying mind and body

Relaxation is like preparing the soil for planting the seeds of your growth and health. Imagine removing large rocks of resistance from your garden and then preparing to plant the seeds of insight and guidance for your life.

Soften your eyes, slowly focus on your breathing, and feel the warmth of relaxation moving through your body. Consciously release any tensions as you become aware of them. Mentally move through your body, picturing and relaxing your toes and feet, calves, thighs, buttocks, abdomen, chest, shoulders, arms, hands, jaw, face, and scalp. Replace any tightness you feel with thoughts of warmth and the steadiness of your breath. Place your attention on the breath as it enters and leaves your body. Be mindfully concentrated on your breath entering and leaving your body.

Open to your intuitive sense. The intuitive function consists of a subtle and mysterious pattern of thinking and sensing. Its organizing function works best when you are relaxed. At first, just sitting and not doing something physically may feel challenging and stressful. Your mind may be restless and flighty as it moves from one running monologue to another. You may be bouncing like a ball from one association to another, from one sensation to another. It may feel as if your inner intuitive voice has nothing to say that day. That's fine. Please think of this as a time each day to shift your attention from the outer world to your inner, intuitively sensed world and allow things to take their shape.

You are allowing the quiet to form within you
so you can experience any thoughts or feelings that may occur.

Step 2: Visual thinking—giving yourself a road map
You can add visual images and words from this quiet place, with your intuition connecting you to a fuller perspective. Consciously choosing pictures and thoughts, you use them to follow new paths and to experience insights into problems and possibilities. Although I present visualizing following by affirming words, the reality is that you will usually find yourself doing both simultaneously. Like reading a picture book, you see and hear the words simultaneously.

In your inner reality, you can use purposeful imaging to experience precisely what you want to experience in your outer reality, including the exact behaviors and attitudes you would like to create for any given situation. For example, you can picture yourself calm and fully aware as you mentally live through your moment-to-moment life. You can imagine your results and the process of attaining your goals. Try creating mental movies, poems, or prayers. Think of making a map that stretches from where you are now to where you want to go. Imagine experiencing your goals fully attained, with an appreciation for your accomplishments. Be playful with your mind.

Allow yourself to think radical thoughts.
Sometimes, you have a specific target goal and know the visual sequences you want to imagine. This may be a health goal, a relationship, a new learning skill, or attitude maintenance. With specific target goals, visualize your ideal outcomes as vividly as possible and see the result existing in the present, not the future. At other times, you will just let your natural sense take you. Use the image of a road map, which points the way to a destination and provides options for getting there.

If your destination is freedom from an illness, you will no doubt want to focus on some images of health. For example, you may imagine yourself walking free from pain, having dinner with the family around the table with everyone sharing a laugh, climbing a hill overlooking the lovely landscape, or all those things. Inner journeying requires only your mind's awareness.

Step 3: Affirming—articulating through directed word power
Word power works directly with visual thinking; they are partners. Language is a powerful tool, internally and externally, creating consciousness and memory. To articulate in words adds power and structure. It takes the images and translates them so that they make sense to the language-oriented part of your brain. You are adding the storyline to your pictures or, if you prefer, pictures to your storyline. In both ways, these partners form the action steps toward a goal. Along with the action, you are also choosing a new internal dialogue based on your own self-determination. Whenever you name something, it makes it more real.

Affirmations are declarations of your intentions and destination—statements to your conscious mind that the things you think and visualize are really possible for you. You want them to be emotionally felt to help nourish the seed you are planting in your mind.

You give yourself positive inner language by clearly articulating your direction, action steps, and desired attitude.

Begin affirming while you are imaging or imaging while you are affirming. The combination holds the power of your intentions impressed upon your mind. For example, while you are still visually thinking, form words or phrases that reflect your full potential and give you direction. And remember that while you're focusing on living a life with meaning, it's wise to include your ideals, purposes, and values—not those of others. These are *your* road maps, pointing to the direction in which *you* are heading and the potential *you* wish to fulfill. As you hold these words and images in your mind, know that they have the power of your conscious and intuitive mind behind them.

You will strengthen your desired direction and mental road map by creating a simple drawing or visual symbol (remember the simplicity of a circle, square, or arrow). We remember words more easily when we pair them with a picture or symbol.

Close with Self-Acknowledgment
Open your eyes to come back from the stillness to the outer world. Acknowledge yourself for having slowed down to devote this time and

energy to your personal development, problem-solving, health, and well-being. Remind yourself that you are in training, moving toward the highest and best you can offer yourself. You choose to change and grow, granting yourself time to rebalance and focus with purpose and direction.

*Know that you face the world with more resources
and insights now than you had a few minutes ago.*

Does this mean all your problems at work and home will be over? No. But you are working on your ability to handle them with the best attitude and sense about yourself. You are in mental training—you hope to live in creativity and total fulfillment, even if in the moment you may be hanging on as best you can within a particularly challenging situation. If this is the case, then be gentle with yourself. Hanging on and coping may be the most creative and heroic task possible.

Personalizing Your Approach

Some people see their inner workout as the most dynamic and creative period of their day; others see it as the most relaxing time. Some people like a more extended relaxation period and take extra time to enjoy that peaceful, intuitive place within themselves. Others relax for a shorter time and go immediately to more directed visual thinking and word-powered affirmations. Some prefer to sit at their desks for a few minutes of introspective reflection. I enjoy the quiet, using most of my inner mind session for relaxing, adding images and words at the end to clarify and affirm my direction, intentions, and attitude. People learn to develop their own rhythm and style of reflection. No way is "wrong"—or even "more right" than another.

*The important thing is your daily commitment
to be reflective with yourself.*

After a short while on your inner fitness program, you may find daily difficulties and stresses will not overwhelm you as often as before. You will be better able to detach and develop a new perspective. Your attitudinal muscles are stretched to greater capacity, allowing you to aim for goals that previously seemed beyond your reach. You will feel more balanced and empowered. You discover insightful new ideas blossoming. It is not a panacea but learning a new, enlivening perspective on life.

A Mind Fitness Meditation for Personal Peace

I walk out into a lovely backyard garden scene. The flowers are well groomed, with bright blossoms of gold and deep blue forming a circle around a hammock stretched between two giant oak trees. The air is warm, and there is a mild breeze. I walk along a small path through the blue and yellow flowers and up to the hammock, where I lie down and stretch out in perfect trust and comfort.

I gently rock myself back and forth in the hammock and draw deep, full breaths of quiet joy and peacefulness. I hear birds singing their songs of gladness. With each breath, I become more at peace, more at peace with myself and my surroundings. The warm, clean air washes over me and through me. I am serene and entirely at peace.

Your Mind Fitness Booster Exercise

Take a few moments now to run through the elements of a Mind Fitness session.

- Prepare by doing a few quick stretches.
- Get into a comfortable posture by sitting or lying straight.
- Align yourself with your intuitive spirit by being mindfully open to the inner quiet.
- Relax, releasing mental and physical tensions, taking long, slow breaths. Focus inwardly and become open to your intuitive sense.
- Visualize an image of being exactly as you would like in today's world. What values do you hold as important? What are you doing? Who is around you? Stretch your imagination to see the ideal.
- Affirm in words that you can achieve your goal by saying, "I am creating that now."
- Close with a moment of self-acknowledgment; thank yourself for taking a few moments to try something new and healthful.

In the next chapter, I will go more fully into how to relax the body and mind and the nature of the intuitive sense.

Chapter 7

Stop, Relax...

Relaxation is a human need—physically, mentally, and spiritually.

Relaxing

WHAT A CONFLICTED idea relaxation is for us Americans. We are an active and somewhat driven people with a Puritan heritage that encourages constant productive activity.

When I lived in Europe, it became very real to me just how foreign the idea of relaxation is to Americans. Americans seemed to want to work around the clock, frowning on all the European vacation days. It became apparent that many of us had never learned the skill of relaxation. We needed to learn how to stop and take advantage of the mandatory downtime many European nations require by law.

Americans tend to see the Eastern idea of doing one thing at a time or sitting quietly as wasteful. Sitting and doing nothing? Pausing? We respect those who do two or three things simultaneously to feel productive. What a leap it takes for us to say and believe:

I am taking the time to sit down and relax now because I know it is good for me. It brings me pleasure and peace of mind and is vital for my body and spirit. As I silence my mind, my breathing becomes deeper and fuller, my heart beats slower, and I can feel my muscles loosening, reaching a place of inner peace.

(The italicized meditation running throughout this chapter appears again in a complete sequence in Chapter Twenty-Five.)

So what exactly is this elusive thing called "relaxation"?
Webster's Dictionary defines relaxation as "a rest from work" or "recreation." Recreation is "refreshment in body and mind," and recreate is "to restore, refresh or to create anew." During your Mind Fitness sessions, you are mindfully quieting yourself, "turning off" the outside world, and going within to recreate your thoughts, attitudes, and life perceptions. You mentally create the actions and attitudes that allow you to contribute to your life fulfillment and potential. This re-creating takes root in the soil of inner quiet, in the peaceful rest of mind and body. There is unification within your very being.

Relaxation is the soil in which we plant our future seeds.
I feel that presence of wholeness, beauty, and total tranquility. The bubble of spirit rises up, giving new meaning to everything I had been worried about during the day. This clear bubble is a quiet feeling that unifies my body, mind, and heart. I exhale, and my muscles and mind relax.

Medical science now links prolonged physical and emotional tension to illnesses, including ulcers, asthma, and spastic digestion. The body, when stressed, loses some of its ability to fend off viruses and chemical stresses. Thus, researchers are giving increasing attention to how relaxation contributes to health. Who would have thought that relaxation, mindful meditation, and reflection would be essential health boosters? We now realize that body, emotion, mind, and spirit come together naturally when relaxed. At that point, the body can begin to heal and replenish itself.

Relaxation occurs naturally as you experience your breath flowing in and out of your body. Relaxation eases tension and calms the constant activity in both your body and mind. The more subtle forms of experiencing and thinking from your intuitive intelligence can now occur.

I draw in another deep and full breath, shifting the breathing from my chest to my ribs and lower abdomen. I breathe in again deeply, expanding my rib cage as I hold the air in my abdomen for a few moments and then slowly let it out. I feel the richness of the moment alive within me. I allow the quieting to move through my chest, back, stomach, and lower intestines, then down through my groin, legs, and feet, relaxing and letting go of all tension.

Peaceful Place

It is always easier to relax when you are in a comfortable posture and peaceful place. This allows you to feel a sense of calmness and inner peace. The setting may be as simple as under a tree, in your car, in your favorite armchair, or on a floor cushion. You want to be in a place where you feel safe and uninterrupted and your body does not feel tension.

As I take another full breath, I feel the increased oxygen circulating through my body and brain. I call on the power of my concentrated mind to focus on one thing and hold that point. I will focus on an image of a peaceful pond with a big shade tree on its shore, with cattails and other reeds growing around it. The pond is serene. There are no ripples on its surface. It is entirely tranquil. I inhale a sweet scent, filling my mind with images of this pond. I let go of any other thoughts I may have, focusing on the tranquility of my mind and emotions and the relaxation of my body.

You ultimately focus on reaching a special place *within* yourself, a place of relaxation and mindful insight, from which you mentally quiet your thinking. It is helpful to have a designated mental place that you think about when you want to relax deeply. I have several model relaxation spots where I mentally begin my relaxation time. One is a waterfall I have known for years in Hawaii. I also like to lie down mentally in the hammock on my friend Dave's lawn as I did years ago or in the back of my dad's sailboat as I did as a child, watching the water lap against the hull. These are places and moments in which I was conscious of feeling very relaxed and at peace within myself.

Sometimes, I mentally focus on being in a meadow on a spring day; other times, I see myself walking down the beach with the waves lapping at my feet. I feel immediately more relaxed and rested because I can realistically recall the experience of peace and serenity that I felt while there at one time or another. I build from that remembered sense of quiet to a renewed sense of relaxation and calm within myself.

Learning to Relax

Relaxation and sleeping are not the same. Relaxation means freeing the body and mind from unnecessary tensions and distractions and allowing them to quiet, balance, and recharge while remaining alert and awake. Sleeping is, well, you know—a state of unconsciousness. When we sleep, we are "shut down," unaware of many outward sensations and events. In contrast, when we are in an active state of relaxation, we are focused on being aware of the present moment. We are fully alert but calm and restful simultaneously.

As novel as the idea may sound, you want to watch yourself rest. You are an observer of your own body and state of mind. You do not need to worry about becoming unconscious or hypnotized in any way during a relaxation session. You are calm and quiet but fully alert and in control.

During your relaxation session, be willing to create an internal environment that will allow new thoughts to come to you. With expansion thinking, there is a reframing of old problems and stalemates that enable new insights to release you. Events in your life and the lives of others can often be seen in fresh ways. You want to create the body and mind calmness that allows for those fuller insights and even moments of forgiveness. It is not so much a matter of adding new things into your life as it is about dropping old opinions of who you are or what you have been through. You grow out of one thought and into a fuller one.

Consciously relaxing allows you to drop old tensions and perceptions. It offers a release similar to de-tensing a muscle in your arm or leg. As you focus your attention and release your hidden arm and leg tensions, you also open the doorway to releasing long-held opinions and attitudes. You may discover shadow attitudes you weren't aware of, much as you were unaware of the tension you may have been holding in your arms and legs.

My mental picture of my relaxed body is that of a sleeping cat, totally at peace with the world, purring in its most contented way, with no tight muscle anywhere. My body becomes like a cat's—loose, limp, totally at one with the world around me. My body feels heavy as I release any desire to move or hold on to anger.

Muscle Relaxation Exercise

One of the first things to learn is how to tell the difference between held-in muscle tension and muscle relaxation. Let's start to be aware of the differences within the body.

Take a moment to squeeze all your muscles in your arms, legs, torso, and neck. Tense your whole body, counting to 5. Now release your right hand on your lap. Mentally tell yourself to relax your right arm and focus your attention there. Feel the muscles grow a bit heavier and release. Now, try it with your right leg. Mentally concentrate on relaxing and de-tensing the muscles in your right leg. Focus first on your thigh as you release the muscle tension, then work your way down to the knee, ankle, and foot muscles, feeling each area grow heavier as you release the held-in muscle tension. Now, consciously relax your arms and legs, feeling them grow heavier as they settle.

Giving Ourselves Permission

Learning to relax consciously is a skill we, as adults, may want to learn and practice. It is not something that comes out of the blue. Babies have it—see how they loll in a contented, utterly relaxed posture. But as we mature, we begin to hold tensions. We are all creatures of habit and emotions, including how we hold our muscle tensions. So, getting those muscles to de-tense requires a bit of new mental focus. You can do this by just focusing your attention on your physical body, squeezing all your muscles tight and then telling yourself to relax, experiencing a shift in tension.

Most importantly, you want to give yourself permission to relax. Remind yourself that in this techno world, we've learned that pausing for a few minutes daily, consciously relaxing body and mind, and moving from the external to the internal mind is one of the healthiest things we can do for ourselves.

The Breath

The breath entering and leaving your body, slowly and deeply, is the physical means to trigger a relaxed state. Try yawning; open wide and, as you breathe in, let the breath fill your lungs, fully expanding your rib cage. As the breath moves to your lower abdomen, hold it for a count or two, then slowly release the air in a long, steady stream as you feel your rib cage releasing. Repeat this process—filling the lungs, followed by slow rib expansion into your abdomen—three to five times and feel how your body naturally begins to release the stress and tension from its muscles. Tension leaves your body during each exhale. Some people exhale through the nose, and others through the rounded lips of their mouths. Both work well to stimulate relaxation. Again, feel free to exhale in the way you are most comfortable.

As I take a deep breath, I feel the flood of quietness reaching every part of my body. I imagine a golden, honey-colored light pouring down through the top of my head. I feel the release as the light touches my eyes, melting all the tension down my cheeks and through my mouth, throat, and neck, inviting me to give in to its warmth and release the tightness in my shoulders, arms, wrists, and fingertips.

Deep breathing can help eliminate excess muscle tightness at any time, quickly, and without drawing particular attention to yourself. Try it while waiting for red lights to change, waiting in lines, riding in elevators, or when you are on hold on the telephone.

A relaxed state shifts your attention from the outer world to your inner source, restoring your physiological and psychological balance and giving you a chance to rest.

Allow your breathing rate to slow down and deepen as you consciously release tension in all body parts. As you quiet and release the chatter of thoughts, you will feel calm and serene—at peace with yourself and the world. You become a self-listener and a seer. This is the place of power where your intuitive sense can be experienced, and your images are most effective, where they can affect what happens in your life.

In this alert yet restful, mindful state of awareness, you are most open to understanding the larger patterns in your life. This leads to deep listening and looking, which brings about insightful and intuitive thoughts. You can develop in a way you cannot when responding to outside pressures. You are quietly still, not moving around doing things. Your eyes are usually lowered or closed. Your attention is focused inward, on the breath and sensations you may become aware of within your body.

In much the same way as you might say to a child who wants to tell you a story, "Wait until I can sit down to really listen to you," you need to take time out and consciously relax to sense your potential and belief in yourself. This is a time to sit and listen to what we might call "your Soul talk."

Chapter 8

So Now... Invite the Intuitive

Relaxation lets you experience your larger intuitive sense.

W HEN YOU'RE ROUNDING up the kids at the last minute and loading them into the car, or when you're frantically looking for a parking place or jockeying for a position of power around the conference table, you're rarely in touch with your intuitive sense. The intuition speaks in a whisper.

People have said to me, "Intuition? I don't feel anything!"

"A voice? What inner voice?"

The inner voice is your self-talk, derived from your intuitive sense, gut-level feelings, hunches, and insights. We all have gut hunches that encourage us to do something or another. Your intuition is your internal radar. When you think not out of ego or fear, you may be in touch with that broader sense that we call intuition.

A fuller understanding comes from joining the conscious and unconscious mind, weaving a complete pattern of recognition and awareness. It is an intelligence that senses a more comprehensive picture than the five physical senses. Your inner voice, your thinking, takes in a whole perspective. Small daily demands or personal beliefs do not detract you. It is your unique sense of what is called the Divine. Most people's fuller understanding deepens their natural inclination toward interconnection and wholeness. Unknown wisdom comes to us sometimes—in a flash, without explanation, or more slowly, as a growing sense of wholeness and profound thinking. This wider intelligence seems to kick in when the outer senses are quieted and the mind is quietly focused. By closing your eyes, you hear better, feel more sensitively, and taste more completely. Once you feel that inner quiet, you can use your mental faculties to clarify and impress upon your conscious mind a larger pattern of inner knowing.

I am taking time to reflect daily to improve my health and well-being and welcome new thoughts and feelings that benefit me and others. This is when I can fill my mind with thoughts of fullness, of my dreams for myself and the world. When my mind rests quietly, it also becomes aware of insights and creative ideas—pictures, sensations, or words.

During this time, let yourself think about ideals and possibilities. Allow your thoughts and visions to go beyond limits to larger, interdependent, and connecting levels. With your barriers down, the idealized sense of what is right and true can find a voice within your mind. Your "genius within" may answer puzzling questions with a flash of insight. Its answers are not worded in "shoulds." Other people and your culture tell you what you "should" be doing in a particular situation. Regarding personal life goals, your intuitive intelligence helps you become aware of what *you* need for your own wholeness. This fuller understanding comes from deep inside, not outside expectations and sources.

I take another deep breath, knowing I have taken time to reflect, nourish myself, and connect my body and spirit. I understand that this inner time helps my body heal, that my mind and emotions reach a point of clarity, and that my spirit touches the source of life.

In a relaxed state, listening to your inner self, you may suddenly get a solution to a problem you have been pondering in your normal state of mind for some time. In Rollo May's classic book, *The Courage to Create*, he points out that these answers often come right after you focus intensely on the problem with your conscious mind and then let it go. When you put aside the intensity of your search and begin to move into a state of relaxation with focused listening and looking, the answer often pops right into your mind, like a bubble to the surface. Most of us have had the experience of waking up in the middle of the night with a new idea or way of approaching a situation. The deeper mind works with this letting go.

People often ask, "How do I know whether it's my real inner intuitive sense or just some good idea my ego came up with?" The best indication is that the intuitive insight is usually quiet. It whispers rather than yells (unless it's an emergency).

***The ego's voice is loud, repetitive, and pushy,
while the intuitive voice is usually calm, gentle, and insightful.***
You can work a lifetime for the goals other people dictate to you and even achieve great success. But you will only be truly happy, delighted, and fulfilled if you have reached within and found out what you really want to do as your personal creative expression and contribution.

***Focus your intentions in this state of quietness
for clarity about how to live your life, solve problems,
and best contribute to your soul dance for happiness and well-being.***

A Reflection

The intuitive function can be stimulated with contemplative questions that will only be answered after some time. Such questions might be:
- What am I seeing and feeling about the next step in my life?
- What do I feel is vital to me as I live my daily life?
- Do I have a purpose or destiny in life? What is my soul dance?
- How are my relationships doing? Are they alive? Are they stagnating? Are they fun? Do they expand my thinking about my abilities?
- Are there any unhealed areas that might be affecting my health? What might they be?
- How could I heal those unhealed areas?
- What can I do to forgive a person I feel anger toward? Is there a way to reframe my present angry situation?

- How can I move away from resentment? How can I alter that feeling?
- Are there greater possibilities within me that I want to bring out?
- What are the lessons I might be learning? What keeps coming up?

I know a man who had a brilliant career as an attorney but was never really inwardly happy or at peace until he began to play music for some time each day. That music became his source of deep personal expression, a pleasure fulfilling him meaningfully. It was part of that richer and deeper interconnection that whispered to him, and he came to feel intuitively that it was a part of himself.

A central theme of this work is permitting intuitive intelligence to be felt by making specific times when you stop all your other activities and mindfully relax in the quiet.

I take another deep breath and release any tension my body may still be holding. I reflect again on a pond with its quietness—the beauty of the water's reflection, the green tree's fullness, and the reeds' gentleness as they grow near the water's edge.

I feel myself awakening to the reality around me. I begin to wiggle my fingers and toes, take a deep breath, slowly open my eyes, and feel refreshed and unified in body, mind, and heart, knowing that I did something good for myself today.

Focus Questions

Listen to (or read) the introductory Mind Fitness session for relaxation. The full text can be found in Chapter Twenty-Five. Take a few deep breaths and begin to relax. Feel your muscles releasing their tension. Feel a sense of peace flow over you. Enjoy the quiet.

After you are relaxed and mentally at peace, reflect on some open-ended focus questions. A good focus or leading question requires us to respond with more than just a quick "yes" or "no." It demands more thought and self-examination. You may decide to think about these questions for months, allowing them to come and go in your consciousness.

- What is essential to me? What do I value?
- What do I want to actualize?
- What do I think is possible?
- What do I think is impossible?
- What are my limitations, if any?
- What internal resources and skills do I think I will need?
- What outside resources and skills will I need?
- Can I imagine something affecting the outcome?
- What, if any, may be the consequences of this?
- Is there a downside? What's the worst that can happen?
- Am I prepared to make mistakes and then still go on?
- How do I generally handle mistakes?
- What have I learned from my mistakes? From my successes?
- After attaining success, how will I feel?

Chapter 9

"Look"—Visual Descriptive Thinking

*"It's amazing what one can accomplish
when one doesn't know what one can't do."*
~Garfield, the cat

YOUR MIND IS a canvas—you get to experiment and play. Close your eyes and paint an imagined red apple in the middle of a white canvas in your mind: You mentally paint an image. We do this all the time when we remember what something looks like. After a short while, that single picture you had on a canvas might expand into a video replaying how you drive home or you as the hero of your own life. Your video can show you doing what you want and being the way you want to be in your life. Your movie can be of you successfully living your values.

Focused visual thinking allows you to paint or imagine using mental pictures consciously. It is a personal, deep-centered, and active process. Visualizing is a multi-sensory task not limited to the inner mind's sight. As you grow more experienced with visualizing as a tool, you will be able to create the feeling of actually being someplace, doing whatever you are imagining, in your mind's eye. That is how athletes practice their sport in their minds.

Don't be taken aback if you are one of the many people who say they "cannot see anything." You may visualize more with your emotions or sense of hearing or touch. You may experience smells and sensations such as temperature changes. You may not be able to see a red apple in your mind exactly, but you can *sense* that apple when you think about it. You have a sense of its size, taste, skin, and seeds. Visualizing involves becoming internally aware.

Emotionally balanced and healthy people lean toward mentally painting images and goals that enrich their self-esteem—that direct and support their life successes. One woman with a strong sense of self explained, "When I am resting, I imagine myself talking and enjoying a relaxed day with my family and friends." Another woman, caught in a hostile, harmful, addictive thinking pattern, imagined anger, fear, guilt, or self-deprecating images. "I obsess on yelling at my sister, telling her all the reasons I am angry with her."

Which of the above women do we expect to be leading a happier life?

We get what we consciously aim for,
so let's aim where we want to go.

Some of your visual thinking will be intuitive, allowing images to float into your mind. Intuitive visual thinking creates pictures or sensations from your unconscious, making them more available to your awareness. Other images you will consciously evoke through focused visual thinking—purposefully creating an experience in your imagination from several different perspectives, using as many senses as possible: sight, hearing, touch, smell, and taste. These kinds of inner images come from the intuitive and the conscious intelligence. Both are potent guideposts. Both types of visual thinking involve thinking descriptively as if watching a movie or reading a book.

Visual thinking is a core part of whole-brain learning.

Imagination and Fantasy

I couldn't write about visual thinking, imagination, and intuitive intelligence without mentioning the pioneering psychoanalyst Carl Jung. Jung believed fantasy to be a vital component of a healthy person's life. Through fantasy, we can play out the ideas and elements of life in our minds and alter and reshuffle the possibilities. We are free to juxtapose the oddest combinations—imagination has no limits.

Jung wrote: "But what great thing came into existence that was not first fantasy? All the works of humanity have their origin in creative imagination. Fantasy is a natural and vital activity which helps the seeds of development to grow." Fantasy is essential to knowing ourselves.

*Any life goal you want to aim for
consciously must first exist in your conscious mind.*

- Identify: The first step, using the personal development cycle, is to identify one specific thing you want to change.
- Acknowledge: The second step is to acknowledge and accept that you want to change in this way to be the person you want to be. You acknowledge that you wish to make this change a new focus.
- Create the change: The third step is to create the change you want by actively imagining and acting upon that change.

How can we ever think we can reach a goal unless we aim consciously in that direction? We can find ourselves in a downward spiral without being conscious, but to reach our full potential, we must become increasingly aware of the images and self-talk we engage in.

*It comes down to making choices and deciding how you
want to live within each moment to reach your ultimate goal.*

When you proactively imagine attaining your goal, you are mentally focused, using your imagination in a predetermined way. You are living out—mentally and emotionally—your passions, achievements, fears, and waves of anger. You can discover what you are thinking and feeling when you take the time to check in with yourself and watch where your quiet takes you. What are you thinking these days? It makes sense that the time you spend visualizing yourself doing your best helps you act in that direction.

The far-thinking educator John Holt echoes Jung: "Action begins with fantasy. We are very unlikely to do something new, difficult, and demanding until after we have spent some time imagining or dreaming of ourselves doing it."

Am I suggesting you spend all your life in unrealistic fantasies? In visual magical thinking? No, it's another potent thinking tool we can use to our benefit if we choose to learn how. Our brain offers this tool if we wish to activate it.

A Translation Process

A translation process happens as you move your thinking from vague desires and thoughts to the real thing. We all want to live better, at least in the abstract. But what does "living better" really mean to you? Take a break for a moment. Ask yourself a question or two, and then close your eyes. Try a little "movie watching." Use your imagination as you seek the answers.

- How can I live my life with greater satisfaction and well-being?
- Where do I want to be in two years? Five years? Two days? Two hours?
- If I had all the money I needed, what would I do with my time?
- What must I feel to experience good health and mental balance?
- What would make me deeply peaceful at this moment? In a day? In a month?
- How do I fit in…to my family, community, and life?

Ask these "getting to know me" questions and watch what pictures and feelings come to mind. Create an internal environment where you can get to know yourself as you focus on your potential, translating abstract values and desires into detailed goals and concrete action plans. The more you can mentally experience your real and imagined successes, the more precise you grow in defining—and reaching—your concrete goals.

Once you see your dreams become actual plans, you can set your priorities. You will naturally use your mind to sequentially arrange the required steps and details—mapping out a route to attain your goals. You'll see how they fit into the larger picture of your life. Your thinking moves from "I want that" to "I know how to achieve that."

__As you imagine your goal becoming real, you will refine it on an ongoing basis. Don't rush it; it has a rhythm all its own.__

From Dream to Reality

My daughter's friend dreamed of living in Hawaii and going to school. At first, it was nothing more than a teenager's dream, but as she spoke of it more and more often with excitement and expectation, she saw her goal more clearly each time. She developed a passion for making this idea happen. As she imagined herself there, she saw how it would fit into her goal of attending university. Then, she made it concrete by sequencing the steps needed to take action. Her dream goal became more attainable and tangible as she completed each action step. The move to Hawaii took her a little longer than she expected, and she missed her September target date, but she got into the community college and the dorm by mid-year. This is a beautiful example of a goal achieved. An example of imagining something with enough intent, passion, and, very importantly, the will for action so that she could focus clearly enough to turn her life goal into a reality.

The Power of an Image

One woman related how she had been trying for a long time, during moments of stress and uncertainty, to live the slogan "Let go and let God" as her way of affirming her trust in everything turning out okay. Recently she formed the image of God as a pair of hands in which she placed herself and her loved ones and the day's stresses. She felt held. "Having the visual image of a pair of hands made all the difference in the world to me. It somehow allowed me the faith to be able to let go and trust in God. Whenever I begin to worry again, I see the hands and mentally place my concern into them. It feels more trustworthy to me somehow to see something I recognize."

Asking the "What If?" Possibility Question

By asking "What if?" questions with an open imagination, you begin to observe your thinking style. You may notice your mind repeatedly creating the same unhelpful thought or beating you down with various forms of disrespect. As we all know, when we are stressed, our thinking is down; everything looks irritating and negative.

We often find it easier to ask ourselves "What if?" questions from fear, anger, and upset. What if this lump is cancer? What if I could tell them off? But how about doing an "about-face" by totally changing directions, asking yourself positive, uplifting "What if?" questions? This is stretching the old imagination upward! You might find that your mind has difficulty going there because it always wants to return to the old familiar *negative* "What ifs?" When you notice that happening, gently remind yourself of your new exercise and bring those wanderings back to the Up Side of the process. What if this lump is *not* cancer? What if I just relaxed over the situation? What if I had it checked and found out for sure?

Are you ready to practice greater possibilities?

One of the most notable changes comes when you ask yourself, "What if?" and quietly focus on the most ideal options imaginable. Stretch and push your limitations in unrestrained possibility thinking.

- How would that look?
- What changes would be made?
- What would you do differently?
- What would show you, without a doubt, that you were happier?

Most of us are so busy asking fearful "What if?" questions, perceiving negatives, fears, upsets, and disappointments, that we forget to ask optimistic, happy "What if?" questions. It's a mind game of expanding your possibilities, of outrageous thinking. If you cannot conceive of your happiness, it's tough to create it…whatever the "it" may be in your life at the moment. Take a moment to use your visual thinking to actively imagine and see the answers to these positive thinking questions. What would that really look like of you? See it and say it to yourself.

Ask yourself:
- "What if" all my frustrations at work were to be solved?
- "What if" I suddenly had no more financial concerns?
- "What if" my health was fully restored to optimal? What would that mean to me? How much more could I physically do that I don't do now?
- "What if" everything was going great?
- "What if" I was to smile at everyone I met today?
- "What if" I was to meet up with someone I enjoyed today?
- "What if" I was happy even when I had tons to do?
- "What if" I stayed mellow even when the kids were too loud?
- "What if" I was to take a walk or a bath and relax?
- "What if" only good things were to come to me today?

You may also notice that when your mind is more optimistic, you see life without limitations or judgment. There's a degree of compassion and gentleness to your perceptions. When you notice your mind in a positive, constructive thought pattern, acknowledge that to yourself. You can affirm that this optimism is how you want to respond more often. Don't be afraid to self-affirm: "Thank you, mind, for staying on the Up Side. Looking good!"

Chapter 10

Self-Talk

"To recognize something as beautiful,
sometimes all it takes is a change of perspective."
~Christian Cooper

Are you talking to yourself again? Yep—you bet. We talk all the time in our heads. The question is, are we talking positively to ourselves? You may often find that critical attitude "dissing" others or yourself in your mental chatter. Having inner peace is hard when mentally tearing up yourself, other people, and things around you.

At first, it may feel like work to focus on seeing possibilities in your life when imagined from a place of success. Closing your eyes and visualizing your ideal attitudes, behaviors, and circumstances may feel strange. Few of us were encouraged to do this as children. You may remember a teacher or parent telling you, "Stop daydreaming!"

They thought you were wasting time in idle thoughts—but they were wrong. Spending time mindfully imagining your life from a place of quiet and wholeness is like filling your car's gas tank—a regular refueling we need to "keep us running." We are a little wiser when we are quiet, less caught up in the daily, momentary "stuff" of life.

A Reflection

Take a breather. Focus for a few minutes on actively stimulating new options and possibilities for yourself. Mentally push the outer edge and think radically outside what is generally expected of you by yourself and others.

Shadows

As you permit yourself to drift in that intuitive, creative, nonlinear mode, you may drift off into thoughts that feel fearful and unknown. You can stop, acknowledge those scary thoughts, and then actively create the ideas you would rather have. Because the imagination is playful and creative, as you begin to exercise it, you may find yourself in places with new images unfamiliar to your present way of thinking. You may be uncomfortable with the new truths you perceive as you tap into new thinking realms.

Exercising this conscious and active imagination means trusting yourself very courageously. It takes courage to allow your mind to drift off into visual images, moving from one association to another as you watch where you wander, actively imagining what things might be like from different points in time, locations, relationships, and consequences. Back to the question: What if…

Within the imagination, the walls defining spirit and shadow can dissolve, leaving you feeling more exposed and more intertwined with both the shadow and the mysteries than before. Your imagination crosses boundaries in a split second, joining options and components you may never have connected before, and you come closer to feelings you've been keeping "safely" distant.

This kind of imaginative spiritual thinking creates new visions of possibilities and actions.

This is an active process of creativity. When Albert Einstein was only 16 years old, in his brilliant imagination, he rode on the tip of a light beam as it sped through space. From this visual mental image, he went on to speculate on the very nature of light, time, and space, expanding new visions of possibilities and closing old separations of reality.

***All far-reaching visions spring from an
active and courageous imagination.***

A Healing Power Story

Here is a story of my first significant personal contact with the power of imagery, prayer, and belief in another's healing. A 28-year-old man named John was referred to me a few years ago. He had been diagnosed with skin cancer three times and had undergone surgery twice. Before he had another operation, he wanted to work on his mental imaging powers. John had a lot going for him because he was sure that his continual cancer recurrence had something to do with his mental outlook. He came to me to work on his skill of visualizing from both the conscious and unconscious mind, which could affect the course of his cancer.

We worked together for six weeks, imaging cancer cells being carried off in a dump truck and then thrown off the face of the Earth. John created an image of himself as a knight in armor, stabbing these killer cells with his long lance and discarding them. We drew pictures, we spoke of what it meant to be healthy, and we prayed together over specific issues of forgiveness that he had regarding his fundamentalist upbringing.

What happened at John's next check-up is beyond rational understanding. He was declared cancer-free and has remained that way for over eight years. He credits the new images he created for himself and the daily time he now takes to affirm his well-being and his choice for health. Every year, he celebrates another year of health with a family party, adding more new images of wellness to his life's storehouse. The speed of his recovery reinforced my respect for the invisible power of the intentional mind.

Mind Fitness Reflection for Overall Physical Health

Several times a day, relax in a chair or lie down and exercise your imagination by affirming and imagining your health in your mind's eye. Visualize yourself as healthy, happy, and in tune with yourself and the world. Practice feeling healthy as often as you can in your powerful inner mind.

I close my eyes and start my inner journey with several deep breaths. This is now becoming a habit I welcome. I begin by looking for any particular areas in my body I should focus on. I wait quietly for a sense of direction.

I now focus my attention on imaging my breath entering my lungs. I see the tiny red corpuscles carrying health and energy throughout my body as they carry life-giving oxygen. I see the health-carrying corpuscles moving from my lungs to my heart and then to my head, brain, shoulders, arms, internal organs, and nerves, through my digestive system, down through my thighs and knees, and out the soles of my feet. For each part of my body, I picture a light of health and a quickening of energy and vitality.

It's essential to be conscious about your imaging and your intentions. If you feel you should pay attention to a particular part of your body, allow your mind to take you there. Feel and see your body, removing anything that's not healthy and life-giving from your system. Focus your healing intentions like a laser beam of positive expectation. You can take as much time as you want with the exercise, doing a quick mind lift, mind booster, or a longer, more detailed workout. If you are physically ill, I suggest sitting or lying down to do a few-minute health booster several times daily.

A Mind Fitness Exercise:
Your Life Goals/An Ideal

Try visualizing your ideals and articulate what happiness means to you in a sentence. Close your eyes and take a few long, slow breaths. Imagine and picture your life if you were thriving and living precisely as you would like. Some people find this somewhat threatening, so be gentle with yourself. Concentrate on the feelings you would be feeling, your attitude, and the sense of inner peace and creative passion you might experience. It is important to feel the emotions and sensations. Focus on allowing yourself to experience a moment of fulfillment.

Reflective Exercise

Write a statement about how you will feel as you focus on creating that "ideal" life. This is a written power symbol of your destination. It may be a sentence such as:

My life is ideal when…

- I have more energy and feel an inner sense of peace.
- I stay aware and mindful in a way that touches all my life's actions.
- I trust my relationships.
- I am doing my work to the best of my abilities.
- I have a good laugh with my coworker.
- I am giving of myself in a balanced and supportive way.
- I take time to connect with my inner Divine.
- I am winning all my games.

It need not be a complex statement. Be simple. Be clear. The important thing is that your statement has deep meaning in your life. Close your eyes and recreate from memory a moment you have experienced. Use that as your model and deeply feel the emotions of such an experience to anchor that specific feeling of fulfillment and peace in your mind and body.

Now, create a visual symbol or image that is meaningful to you to represent your ideal in life in a physical form. This can be a quick squiggle, or you can take time to make it detailed, using different colors. You can also cut and paste magazine pictures. Think of this as a personal crest or life map. You may wind up with several symbols. Try to show visually what is happening for you, inside and out.

Chapter 11

Thinking in Images

One picture is worth a thousand words.

Many people believe that visualization consists of just one kind of imaging, but in truth, there are several forms that we call upon at different times.

1) Memory Images

Let's start with a mental image we all share: ideas formed from memory. They are our familiar, normal life road maps, showing us where and how things should be. They are based on experience and learning, either personally or culturally, and they serve an essential function in our lives.

How would you get along without your memory pictures of where and how things occurred? We use memory images daily: driving around town, recalling directions, remembering where you put something, or even where you live or with whom you are partnered! Memories tell you which employee to call from which office and where to find an instruction manual you filed away. You use memory images to recall how to turn on the computer, what a pine tree looks like, the sound of someone's voice or birds' singing, how a headache or soft touch feels, and the smell of a good cup of coffee brewing. Memory images, using all of your senses, are your primary guidance system as you move through life. We see the all-encompassing traumatic effects of memory loss in those with Alzheimer's, age-related memory loss, or brain injury-induced amnesia.

Here's the problem—old memories trigger old emotions. The problem with this as a way of living is that old memories and emotions usually become so well ingrained that they act as automatic responses or triggers within us. You don't think anew; you respond from the old. The tendency is to react in a predetermined way when confronted with the same stimuli, whether or not it is appropriate today. Knee-jerk reactions are based on past habits rather than a current situation assessment. Those shadow attitudes are throwing temper tantrums. These are the same old insane feelings and moments repeated. It's hard to move ahead when replaying the same old reactions—usually from fear or resentment.

Memory imaging is a terrific skill and essential in day-to-day navigation. Still, you want to realize that operating mainly from memory relinquishes your creative power and potential, relying on old "knee-jerk" reactions. Creating your potential is hard if you operate based only on the past.

You're relying on out-of-date memory images when you fall into the old, limited habits of thought. You are limiting yourself based on old information.

To expand your sense of personal power, you want to become aware of when you are reactivating past thinking patterns or appropriately responding to the situation as it exists today. One man in a business seminar shared that he discovered that whenever he was given a direct order to do something—to work on a project, to meet a deadline—he was reactivating old memories of emotional resistance.

"I would immediately become like an adolescent—defensive and belligerent. A colleague took me to lunch one day after I had blown it during a meeting. He asked me straight out what was wrong with me. After talking it out with him, I realized I was acting just as I did as a kid. It was old stuff. When someone told me what to do as a kid, I would get nasty and rebellious. That doesn't work too well on the job."

A Memory Imaging Exercise

1. Practice creating a physical memory image for a moment. Close your eyes, take a few deep breaths, and mentally see a black ball about the size of a baseball on a white background held at eye level. Hold that image for a few breaths. It takes concentration.

2. Practice visualizing pictures of single commonly known items—a red balloon, apple, or yellow banana—in your mind, then move on to more personal and complex images, such as what your home or family looks like. Add sequencing through time and space by visualizing the route you drive or walk through your home or neighborhood.

3. Next, create a kinesthetic image, feeling movement, such as swinging on a swing or riding a bicycle. Allow yourself to experience the feeling of the image and memory.

2) Creative Images

Creative images allow the mind and spirit to roam in ways that fill you with a great sense of wonder and even humor. They are another form of visual thinking—rather than replaying a real-life memory story, creative images call on the active imagination to paint new pictures of new intentions.

Health and growth require changing—creating something new in your life. It often takes more focus to imagine a picture from scratch than to flash on something that you already know. You are working your active imagination; that means you are putting together unusual combinations of events or subjects. This is a freeing, no-barrier kind of thinking related to daydreaming. This is how you develop creative options.

My old Hawaiian friend, Annie Haleakala, told me that her key to success and happiness in life was that she would "sit back and run pictures in my mind from the best part of myself." She was using creative imaging. It's the difference between coloring in a coloring book with the lines already drawn for you and painting your own creation on fresh paper or canvas.

The latter may take more time and effort initially, but you will sense the rewards from your imagination are well worth it.

A Creative Imaging Exercise

1. To learn how to create new images not based on your experiential memory, take a few moments to see and feel yourself walking on the ceiling, or decorating your office in black and orange, or a cow sleeping in your bed. Just allow yourself to draw as many off-the-wall, incongruent, silly images in your mind's eye as you can. Feel your imagination expanding.

2. Try creating a new kind of perfect pet. Don't be afraid to combine different parts of various animals. Perhaps it has a tail to swing by, wings to fly, an extra-long striped neck, and a pink body. Again, you practice mentally creating something new, so push yourself to allow anything to pop up.

3) Intuitive Images

We are back again to the subtle and elusive intuitive function. Intuitive images are a form of creative imaging that we do not guide. They do not come from the reasoning, guided, imaginative, and intellectual mind but from the world of dreams, inner wisdom, and archetypal knowledge. They are the "hunches" you follow. This form of creative imaging has no specific goal in mind.

Focus on staying aware momentarily,
allowing the breath to enter and leave your body.

Your mind may wander. When it does, focus it back onto your breathing, allowing the mind to empty of its chatter and scatter. In time, you will center yourself enough that, for a few moments, you are open to larger-than-usual ideas. For example, you may have an insight into how you can do something or forgive someone. Open to the wisdom of the moment, from the quiet focus upon the breath. From this state of reflection, images and words rise to the surface of their own will, not unlike the dreaming process.

I like what the English father of contemporary pottery, Bernard Leach, said: "I think the biggest error we have made in evolution is the placing of intellect above intuition. An artist must put intuition first because it is a finer instinct."

An Intuitive Imaging Exercise

To create an intuitive image, sit peacefully, take a few full breaths, and consciously clear your mind. Allow it to grow diffuse or quiet. Allow an idea or feeling to surface. If this is a new mental exercise for you, and you have yet to become accustomed to being aware of your intuition, it may take a little time to learn how to feel, imagine, and listen to your hunches. Have patience.

4) Images with a Purpose

Purposeful images—those images in your mind that you direct like arrows toward a specific and well-defined goal—are creative, too. They are the mental rehearsals you create to help encourage something to happen. You become clear on your destination and aim your thoughts constructively. Does it mean you always get what you are thinking of? Of course not! It simply means you are focusing your mind in that direction and increasing will and determination. Shakti Gawain, author of the early popular book on visualization, *Creative Visualization*, says: "Creative visualization is the technique of using your imagination to create the life that you want."

- The first step in imaging is always to stop and relax. Take a few deep breaths and consciously release all your muscles.
- Now, with determination, instruct yourself to visualize an inner picture of yourself doing something enjoyable. Start with something you know well, such as eating a favorite food or playing a sport you enjoy.
- Detail your visualization with precise, vivid specifics. Use your senses of touch, temperature, smell, and hearing to make it very real for yourself.

Try to mentally imagine yourself running in a meadow on a spring day. Imagine your feet touching the soft ground, the breeze on your face as you run, and your arms moving at your sides in rhythm with your legs. Feel the air entering and leaving your lungs; see the clouds floating in the sky; smell the damp spring grass. Concentrate and actively experience feelings of unlimited freedom and pleasure.

Inner imaging is most effective when you involve all the senses and allow yourself to experience the emotions befitting the moment.

A Purposeful Imaging Exercise

- See and feel yourself doing something you want to be doing: skiing, dancing, taking a peaceful walk, enjoying a close talk with your teenager, being with a loved one, going fishing, doing your job differently, or even getting a job. This is a goal with a specific constructive purpose in your life.
- Create a vivid picture as you would ideally have it. Release any judgments about this exercise not working. Direct the energy using your imaging abilities to target the desired goal and outcome. Feel the experience.

Anchoring Your Goal

Anchor that image and goal of choice. Make any slight movement with intention. Any muscle movement signals a part of your brain to wake up! It makes an impression. If, for example, you want to change a harsh vocal quality to a gentler tone, you'll want to use all your available tools to teach yourself this new behavior. Since we know that mind and body are connected, learning something new can be more easily remembered if we combine the idea with a muscle movement—a reminder from the kinesthetic, physical part of us to stay awake and remember our intentions.

Try making a small gesture when you are intentionally thinking of a goal: touch your hands together, tap your leg, or rub your tongue along the inner side of your teeth as you remind yourself of your intention. You use as many senses and neural connections as possible to make an impression on yourself.

I know someone who touches his watch when he remembers to listen rather than interrupt. Because he is such an enthusiastic person, he often runs over others verbally and then feels guilty for not allowing them their time to talk. He uses a physical anchoring signal to remind himself to "hold back." One tennis pro recommends that his students bounce the ball between plays as they visualize their next serve to integrate the image with the body neurology.

With a Mind Fitness orientation, you are working on learning new ways of thinking to optimize yourself. You want to use as many tools as possible to train your mind and body. Physical anchoring locks the image and idea into your mind with the help of your sense of touch. You become more in control of your perceptions and actions.

A Mind Fitness Imaging Exercise

- Allow yourself a few moments of quiet to become aware of your breath and create an image. If you have trouble, start picturing yourself eating an ice cream cone. See the color, feel the cone in your hand, and taste the flavor. Make it vivid and real while you enjoy every lick.
- Move on to bigger things: Articulate your goals and desires. Look to your dreams. Where are you going? Get a sense of your intentions and potential.
- Use different parts of your imagination: sight, smell, sound, touch, temperature, pressure, speed, emotions, and feelings.
- Imagine yourself living your full potential and sharing the values and attitudes vital to you. What does that look, feel, and sound like to you?

Chapter 12

Affirmation Power

Directed words are powerful.

AFFIRMATIONS ARE SELF-TALK at its finest. The words are positive, upbeat, and directional. They should be clear words that you feel strongly about. A great attitude is "I am clear on my intentions and believe in myself."

We all know people who believed sincerely in their ability to reach their goals and overcame all the known odds. They had an affirming attitude of *no doubt*. This comes from a feeling that you have some control over your life. You believe in your abilities. You are at the opposite pole from victim thinking.

This sense of personal control and trust
in yourself is crucial to mental health.

As you focus on affirming, in words and attitude, you can and will do whatever is demanded when the moment arrives; a new sense of self emerges. You may not have the foggiest idea of what the subsequent circumstance will ask of you, but you trust and believe you will respond to the best of your abilities when the moment comes. You trust you will know the right thing to do at the right time. You are back to the intuitive sense and the belief that it will give you "a hunch" when needed.

Vague Desires

When you affirm, you are being proactive. You are not letting your life slide. You are articulating, in words, initially vague desires such as "I want to be happier," "I want to have more time," or "I want to have better relationships." You give words to what you mentally create in your imagination or visual images to what you first put into words. Remember, the order is unimportant; pairing words and sense images is the key. As you pair these words with visual images, or vice versa, you actively train your mind to focus on the best possibilities and intentions.

These verbal descriptions are compelling. They give language structure to your vague desires, transforming them into reachable goals.

Make an effort to find the right words to fit your true intentions. Choose words that are deeply meaningful to you personally—words that create an impact.

By clarifying your affirmations, you:
- Concisely and clearly state your intention and desired destination.
- Reinforce your belief in yourself and that you can reach your goals.
- Acknowledge who you are in the present.

Directed words empower your direction. Focused self-talk is more than just a feel-good exercise.

How you internally talk or think to yourself definitely influences your perception of reality.

Watch Your Talk

The most negative people are the quickest to say, "All this is just nonsense. Words don't mean anything." In fact, your spoken descriptions greatly influence changing your attitudes and perceptions of life. Affirmations are made up of the language of intention. They help you translate those abstract feelings from your inner mind to the outer world of expressed goals.

For people with healthy and empowered thinking, affirming self-talk becomes a part of their natural thinking process:

- No problem. I can do that.
- I am healthy. I feel good today.
- I accept and believe in my judgment/decision-making/energy/ actions.
- I am keeping my attitude optimistic.
- I choose to think constructively.
- I am grateful for my family and friends.
- I am protective and caring of my health.
- I am glad I am staying cool and calm.
- I am growing more self-assured and in control of my life.
- I am a peaceful/self-assured/easygoing person.
- I enjoy and get along well with others.
- I am in abundance and am grateful for my goodies.
- I am growing more compassionate and loving in my daily interactions.

Acknowledging Real Moments

Since you are working to develop affirmations for yourself, try looking for self-awareness insights in your moments of success and pleasure. The moment you made someone laugh, the moment you felt like you said or did just the right thing, or when you felt proud of yourself. Acknowledging that moment of success and pleasure to yourself is enlivening and self-affirming—very healthy self-talk. Examples include, "I feel good having laughed with him," or "Good for me for saying that to her. My timing was just right."

Look also to your attributes, such as a warm sense of humor, a strong artistic ability, helpfulness and empathy with others, or a moment of courage when you challenge a fear by going through it. You might say to yourself: "I am glad I got through that fear moment," or "I love my artistic abilities; they bring me so much pleasure," or "I got a lot out of helping my neighbor today," or even " Sure did that word puzzle fast!"

Cultivate an attitude of expanded possibilities.

"Thank You! Thank You!"

Did you know you can create a new mental reality through word power before it occurs physically? The clarity of solid intent and feeling encourages you to alter your perceptions and expand your belief structure.

Directed word power statements are like personal prayers. One of the most rewarding affirmations or prayers is "Thank you, thank you!" As I repeat those two words in my mind, I feel such a sense of gratitude for so many things in my life that I instinctively open up to possibilities. This could be true for you, too. When you feel grateful, you ease fears of the future and are open to more enlivening perceptions.

Word power needs time to take hold in your mind. Changing a lifelong pattern of self-talk or an all-too-comfortable behavior or personality trait is not done overnight. You may need to bring yourself back to your spoken intentions many times before thinking about yourself and your potential in those expansive terms becomes comfortable.

You can regularly use supportive and directive affirmations in your internal dialogue with yourself, replacing the criticism, blaming, doubt, and anxiety you feel when overwhelmed and stressed. This is the opposite of conflicted, stressed-out self-talk.

Allow each spoken sentence to work with your internal pictures. Pump some feeling into them, bringing them to life. Make your language structure vivid, detailed, and felt within your heart. This is a very active personal process, which is why it is called *Proactive* Reflection. Proactive entails self-propelled action that is energetic and dynamic.

Let short guiding phrases become something you enjoy.
They show how you treat yourself.
Remember to acknowledge your efforts.

Affirmations and visualizations reinforce the direction and belief that you can do what you intend. They can be significant when you feel yourself slipping back into a behavior pattern you want to break. These little sayings of positive direction can help you re-center and choose the response you want. They're even more effective when you anchor them with a physical movement as a reminder, anchoring your goal.

Language is the symbolic system humans use to create internal organization. It is a significant component of our thinking. After all, human beings are language based. Words act like bookmarks to help us retrieve images and ideas from memory and crystallize future intentions for action.

***Words bridge your inner world of images
and the outer world of physical reality.***

When you combine the power of words with your emotions and firmly focused sensory images, you call upon the "whole brain" power, which significantly increases your power of self-determination.

Advertisers know the power of pictures connected with words. They love to make the public connect a movement or symbol with their slogans. Let's take back this power and create our own "self-advertisements" for our well-being!

A woman trying to stop yelling at her children over little things told me, "I've started using the slogan 'Think' while seeing the sculpture of Rodin's *The Thinker* in my mind. I'm still working on it, but the slogan and image have somehow given me enough awareness and power to overcome some of my yelling habits."

Chapter 13

Two Rhythms, Two Clocks

*"Where I come from, we say that rhythm is the soul of life
because the whole universe revolves around rhythm,
and when we get out of rhythm, that's when we get into
trouble."*
~Babatunde Olatunji (Nigerian drummer)

RHYTHM IS THE timing, the pulse within your cycles and patterns. It is about time. It runs inside and outside of you. It's the clock ticking, and its beat is compelling. Respecting your rhythm has a lot to do with your mental health.

In your Mind Fitness practice, you will discover two rhythms:

Personal Rhythm is being in balance with your own personality style, ability, and motivation. Getting to know your timing takes self-awareness and personal honesty.

Activity Rhythm reflects the demands inherent within each activity. Every activity has a different time requirement. It just takes a certain amount of physical time to do things. Again, honest assessment is needed here.

Looking honestly at our stress, we see that much of it is self-caused. We overbook ourselves mentally, if not physically. We need to be more honest about the time required for many daily activities. How long does it *really* take to answer e-mails/texts, return voice messages, or do homework with the kids?

When I am honest, it does not take me twenty or thirty minutes to shop. It takes me—realistically, from door to door—forty-five minutes, with another ten minutes to unload and put away. Why do I keep telling myself I will be back in twenty minutes to a half-hour? That is wild. It's dishonest and adds stress.

I do the same with emails and texts. Computer work has a rhythm, and I consistently don't allow enough time to do the job, causing myself the stress of underestimating, overbooking, and falling behind.

Rhythm can be thought of as a movement or energy that is repeated several times. You will find that as you reflect quietly each day, you will be better able to recognize your energy cycles, life demands, attitudes, moods, skill levels, and health. You will also be able to evaluate work and relationship patterns better. You will be able to reinforce those beneficial to you and begin to modify others to be more supportive of your intentions.

> ***Rhythm represents the self-evaluation part of Mind Fitness.***
> - **Personal Rhythm** encourages you to look honestly at your energy, habits, and abilities.
> - **Activity Rhythm** asks you to match those abilities realistically to the time and effort needed for the activity.

It's great when the energy requirements of the activity are matched with the person's energy output. It's a flow between the two. For example, Susan has lots of energy and is speedy in her actions and thinking patterns. She finds no trouble completing a particular series of tasks her boss assigns as long as they are not detail oriented. Mary is slower to respond, evaluates everything in great detail, and moves more deliberatively. She finds the same assignment overwhelming in its scope and demands and sees things that Susan overlooks. A manager aware of these individual styles and personality rhythms knows how to request tasks according to each individual's work style. This makes life much less frustrating for the manager and these two employees.

An Exercise in Balance

Close your eyes for a moment, take one breath, and visualize a scale of weights, like the scale of justice. Visualize yourself on one side and your activities and demands on the other. Visualize them the way they feel now. You are probably unbalanced in some way—or you would not be reading a book on decreasing stress to bring more sanity into your life.

Now, visualize the scales growing even as you become aware of your personal and activity rhythms. You can use this as a symbol to help yourself to stay in balance.

Personal Rhythm

We humans each bring together an amazingly odd and different combination of the same elements. We each have individual patterns and cycles—our *modus operandi* in the world.

- Some are more task-oriented; others take a more general, open-ended approach.
- Some rely on their intuitions and feelings to guide them; others go by what they rationally deduce through logic and analysis.
- Some stay up late at night; others are asleep by 10.
- Some prefer to go it alone and are very independent; others socialize and connect with as many people as possible daily.
- Some are more extroverted and assertive; others are more internal and passive.
- Some are auditory, learning best by hearing; others are visual or tactile learners.
- Some are good on short hauls; others are marathon runners.
- Some are quick studies, rapidly assessing a problem and coming up with an immediate solution; others prefer a more analytic, cautious approach.
- Some need a lot of assurance; others are more internally motivated.
- Some fear risk; others thrive on it.

You undoubtedly have an overall sense of your style, timing, impulsiveness, or systematic approach. How would you describe yourself? Fast? Slow? Impulsive? Deliberate? Logical? Intuitive? Emotional? Analytic? Use the above characteristics to give yourself ideas and add your own.

The goal is to match your style with the task you are doing. Only you know when you are in harmony with yourself and when you are in conflict. A deadline for completing a project can spur you on and keep you pumping. Still, a tight deadline—or inadequate preparation or skills—can create enormous internal stress.

- How much stress is creative and energizing for you?
- How much stress is counterproductive?
- Where is your point of unbalance where anxiety kicks in?
- How much uncertainty can you take?

We each have a stress breaking point. Knowing where your point of insanity lies is essential for maintaining sanity. Keep your eye on those critical points between feeling okay, overwhelmed, or out of control. Those points can vary according to the day, your energy, mood, stress level, food intake, exercise level, relationships, kids' health, work level—and just about anything else you can think of. Nothing stays the same, yet there is an overall rhythm and pattern to your personality and way of doing things.

An older woman shared something significant with me one day when she spoke about her rhythm pattern this way:

"Rhythm is knowing what I can and cannot do, what works for me and what doesn't, and how long something will take me. Now that I have lived as long as I have, I am more aware of my rhythms and cycles, my energy and health ups and downs, how I function, what I do easily, what I need to concentrate on, and where I will likely get stuck. I have a deeper, more realistic sense of who I am. I know my patterns. When I was younger, I never knew how to look at myself in terms of different energy levels, rhythms, and cycles."

She had learned her gifts, limitations, and boundaries. Any rhythm or cycle has a pattern. Once you can ascertain your patterns, life becomes much more straightforward. You have a road map instead of wandering around in confusion. That is what daily self-reflection does in your life.

Einstein said that intelligence is seeing the patterns;
sound mental health involves knowing your patterns
and moving with them to the best of your ability.

If we think of stress as energetic rhythms, we might ask ourselves, "How can I create a balance of energy inside and outside of me?" One way is to be honest and realistic about our abilities and the time requirements for the chosen activity.

Values play an important role in personal rhythms and account largely for our choices. Sue was clear on her values. She liked being outdoors, working on a team, and volunteering.

"My values dictate what I like and don't like and what I choose to put my time into. I don't value wine socials, so I don't attend them. I do value ecology, so I go to ecological fund-raisers. Clarifying my values and patterns has helped me consciously create a personally meaningful lifestyle. You probably already have a sense of your likes and dislikes, what you value and do not, and what it feels like when you are in or out of time. What you want to do now is expand that awareness. As you live more aware and balanced, you will naturally grow more in tune with your rhythms and energies.

The practice of inner quieting encourages you to
discover and embrace your rhythms and styles
and incorporate them to your advantage.

Getting into a Mind Fitness Rhythm

Ask yourself when and how you might want to do your Mind Fitness training. Are you a morning or evening person? Do you have a lunch break where you can sit quietly in an office, park, or your car? Do you like to have music playing while you quiet yourself? Do you prefer to spend most of your time relaxing and following your breath in a mindfully aware meditation, or creatively visualizing, or even writing positive intentions and affirmations?

It is essential to identify your rhythms so you can plan to make your inner mind work at the best time and be free from external interruptions. You may not always be able to have everything quiet around you, but you want to create inner quiet inside your mind and heart. You are aiming for a gentle time for yourself. After thinking about her own personal rhythm style, one woman concluded that with her busy lifestyle, her rhythm was that she liked to do her mind training at "different times during the day and night. The only thing regular about it is that I do inner quieting most days, consciously in some way and for some time. I like the inner concentration for my self-reflection."

A Personal Rhythm Exercise

Start to become aware of your different personal rhythms by quietly reflecting on the various tempos and rhythms demanded in your day and generally in your life. Over the next few weeks, actively watch the choices you make. As you become aware of your preferences, you may want to keep a journal, writing or charting your different personal rhythms, values, and cycles. Start with more apparent areas in your life, such as time schedules, work, school, family demands, and other high-priority demands. You will begin to notice a pattern. Here are a few questions to consider as you look over your life and note your preferences.

- What do you prefer to eat and when?
- Are you fast paced or slower moving?
- Do you talk a lot, or are you more on the quiet side?
- Are you highly stressed or more relaxed? How does this vary?
- What times of day are optimal for you?
- When do you feel tired, hungry, restless, or non-energetic?
- What kinds of activities do you prefer?

- Are you drawn to interacting with people, or do you prefer to be by yourself?
- What rhythms do you experience in your general moods and outlooks toward life?
- Do you more often feel positive expectations or dread and isolation?
- Do you actively participate in activities or a form of the arts, or are you a passive observer, preferring to read or watch a movie?
- Do you mostly like being with children, animals, men, women, or elders?

These questions will start you thinking. Remember that being mindful of yourself and your rhythm patterns is a lifelong awareness process.

Activity Rhythm

It is essential to assess each activity and its inherent natural rhythm. Know what you are biting off or facing. There is a difference between the sprint and the marathon—don't confuse the two. The rhythm of golf is different from the rhythm of handball. The rhythm of starting a new hobby is different from the rhythm of running a business. The rhythm of having a baby is very different from that of caring for a dog. All entrepreneurs know there are different energy requirements when starting their own business from those needed when working for someone else.

Your timing analysis helps you avoid becoming discouraged or worn down by thinking something will happen sooner than expected. The cycle of healing from an accident, which requires physical therapy for muscle retraining, differs considerably from recovering from the flu. If you mentally prepare yourself for the long haul, you can better monitor your energy and attitude, keeping your expectations in the zone of reality. As you visualize and affirm your successful completion of various recurring activities, note each activity's timing needs and rhythm. Then, use that knowledge to your advantage.

One teacher who participated in an intensive program to get her administrative license said, "I put a lot more stress on myself because I did not realize the difficulty and the demand cycles that this program would entail. I would have been better prepared mentally if I had understood. Somehow, I could have done it more realistically."

When we misjudge activity demands, timing, and rhythm, we substantially increase our stress and the chances of failure and dropout. Visualizing the overall map of the activity will help you evaluate an overall activity rhythm.

Sit down and focus your analytic intelligence on consciously visualizing the various stages of the activity. Look at all the expected ups and downs, the fast, demanding stretches with the slower times. Run it in your mind like a movie script. Use your imagination and knowledge to create images and timing expectations of the activity.

If you know the long-term rhythm of raising a child, you know that the two-year-old and teenager stages are just rough stages, not lifelong difficulties—despite what you may feel at the time! This broader awareness allows you to better plan and maintain a rational perspective during difficult times. Intellectually knowing something does not guarantee that everything will feel more manageable at the time, but reminding yourself of the big picture is the next best thing. In quieter moments of contemplation, that larger perspective comes into focus and goes a long way toward supporting mental health.

These two workshop comments speak well about the different uses of rhythm:

"In the morning, I spend two to three minutes visualizing my day's known activities and demands. What demands and schedules will I have? Where will I have to speed up, and where can I slow down? This helps me get a sense of my day's rhythm."

"When I think of people, it's been beneficial to me to use the idea of rhythms. I try to understand the energy rhythm between others and me. I have trouble with one man and see red flashes, reminding me to slow down and breathe. With someone else, I have an easy relationship; I see a flow of blue and know I will need less watchful energy there."

When you remember that personal growth and development are lifelong discovery processes, you're less likely to get overly discouraged when things are difficult. Some discouragement is expected at different times; it's part of the human process. Understanding your energy requirements gives you one more tool to help you through those difficult times.

When I listen to music—classical or jazz in particular—I hear the rhythms increase, growing more intense, followed by a slower pace before the music speeds up again. I similarly envision my rhythm pattern in life.

Understanding that you are growing on the inside is a great gift. This long-term orientation helps you to become less discouraged and impatient with yourself when the rhythm pattern is "out of sync" and the stress is up.

An Activity Rhythm Exercise

Evaluating an activity rhythm in your life means being consciously aware of the various stages inherent in its cycle. Start with an activity within the routine of your day, the sport you play, or a relationship rhythm. Starting with something you know well makes it easier to perceive its rhythms. Slowly use visual and descriptive thinking to go through the stages, like mentally rehearsing a movie script. Experience the slower and more demanding moments, times you feel in control, and times when you may feel more stress. See colors, energy rhythms, and patterns. Teach yourself to think in this new way.

Tapping out the rhythm of music and dancing are great ways to become more aware of your rhythm as with the changes of rhythm within the music. Try tapping along with an African or Caribbean drumming recording to feel it.

Adding a Third Rhythm: The Patterning Rhythm

I want to add a third rhythm here. We know that repetition and the power of association help move us into different mental states. Musical or vocal rhythm patterns have a strange and wonderful way of triggering and anchoring new learning. Certain sounds, smells, sights, and other environmental factors can trigger certain feelings to help you work more effectively and effortlessly.

What kind of environment promotes learning and change in you? Play the same music, read the same inspirations daily for a month, and see how you feel. Your body and mind may be triggered to move more quickly into a state of relaxation. Most people find this to be true.

Harry related that his doctor had him use a stress-reduction program. "I like the music on the audio a lot, so I re-taped just the music part and use it as a starter for each meditation session. I can feel my body de-tensing and my mind relaxing as soon as I take the first breath and hear the first minute of the tape. Because I am so familiar with it now, it's connected in my mind with quiet."

A Patterning Rhythm Exercise

If a piece of familiar music could become your quieting relaxation music, try choosing one you really enjoy. See if you find yourself relaxing more quickly as you associate that music with your time for contemplation and rest.

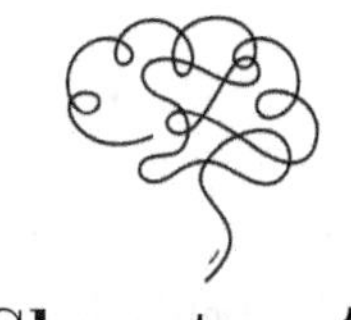

Chapter 14

Mind Lifts Add Clarity

Make your mind lifts detailed and vivid—feel them emotionally.

ONE OF THE most effective methods of focusing your thinking constructively is to flash on a goal image during the day repeatedly. Do a mind lift! Pump that image! Repeat that affirmation of your best intentions. Make a game out of it with yourself.

Mind lifts are brief, constructive mental images or words that help to lift your mind, allowing you to refocus on your goal or recharge your attitude. You may think of a mind lift as a visual slogan, movie scene, prayer, or verse you recite to yourself at any time and place.

Use these short flashes—lasting only a few seconds—of positive thoughts like you would lift a weight at the gym. You are pumping images supporting your intentions, proactively moving your energy in your desired direction.

Repetition Builds Your Bridge

Pumping intentional thoughts is one of the easiest, quickest, and most effective ways to establish new habits and patterns. You can do it almost anywhere, anytime. All you need to do is remember to do it. That repeated momentary flash of positive, creative images can produce excellent results. Remember, you are training your mind—that takes persistence.

By thinking about your statements of intention, you begin to breathe life into them. You repeatedly fill your mind with words and images of your highest intentions and the power of your words. This occurs naturally in anyone who's impassioned: an artist thinks art, a lawyer thinks law, a teacher thinks students, and a mother thinks about her children—each naturally thinks, sees, and replays the most successful strategies for action in their lives. Connections are made among mind, spirit, and body.

Remember, you can affirm silently for clear self-direction.
One manager in a corporate setting told me, "I wrote down five clear self-directions for myself. I now pause and say them silently to myself three times a day. I really like the changes I am experiencing as a result. I feel less reactive and more in control."

Research shows that thoughts produce physical changes in your brain and your chemistry. We are learning that the brain is indeed plastic and that new brain-wave patterns accompany new learning. The more we practice something, the more traveled that neural pathway becomes. Our brain physically changes in response to our new attitudes, skills, and beliefs.

As with mind lifts, you want to repeat your explicit statements of intention often. So use the moments walking down the street, waiting at stop lights, doing the dishes, or whenever you have some "down" mental time you want to enjoy more and put it to good use. This keeps your thinking focused in the direction you want to go.

Backward Speak

Are you looking for results? Watch out for this common pitfall: giving commands by stating what you *don't* want people (or yourself) to do. So often, most of what we say is the opposite of what we wish to say: "Don't go so fast." "Don't be late for the appointment." "Don't spend much money." "Don't eat that ice cream." Children, in particular, have difficulty retrieving the opposite from a statement like that. My favorite example is telling children, "Don't run," rather than the obvious direction of a clear "Walk!"

***Phrase your mental directives in straightforward,
positive ways—they'll be much more effective.***

When we word our directives to others straightforwardly and positively, it's easier for people to act on them. In the same way, better results come more easily when you articulate what *you* intend to *do* rather than what you plan not to do. "I will be there on time" has a stronger intention than "I will try not to be late." Negatively stated intentions force your mind to shift into reverse and find a behavior opposite to what you've said.

"I don't want to be weak any longer" is not the same clear directive as "I am growing stronger and healthier with every breath."

Clarity and intentions differ considerably between "I'll try to read it if possible " and "I will read it today." You want to impress yourself, so don't be afraid to articulate with conviction and force of will. Leave no room for doubt about your intentions. You are clear and focused. Your purpose is strong. And simple words will do just fine:

- "Relax."
- "Take it easy."
- "Trust."
- "Back off."
- "Go slow."

Word Power Guidelines

The guidelines for creating clear affirmations are standard: combine constructive self-talk filled with vivid imagery and strong emotions.

1. Use first-person present tense, even if your goal is not your present reality.

"I am" rather than "I will be." For example, try saying:

- "I am calm and centered" rather than "I will be calm and centered."
- "I am a creative person" rather than "I hope to be creative in the future."
- "I am a resourceful problem solver" rather than "I hope I can figure this out."

When you give yourself directions or reminders, the first-person address is implied.

- "Stop, relax!"
- "Everything is okay."
- "Take a deep breath."
- "Get a grip!"

2. State clearly and positively.

Instead of "I will not lose my temper today," try "I am focused on staying cool and calm today." This is a more straightforward, more vivid message to yourself. Positively worded statements of intention focus on attaining a desired result rather than avoiding a negative one. When you use the word "not," the trickster mind might miss that little "not" word and register it as "I will lose my temper." Then you wonder why you are out of control!

3. Support with solid and positive feelings and emotions.

If you affirm that you are in excellent health, financially stable, or any other value, use your imagination to experience exactly *how* you think that would feel. See your life as a healthy person engaging in active pursuits with pleasure or as someone financially stable and respected for their work. See your surroundings and actions while concentrating on the feelings you would ideally have under these circumstances. Focus on the emotions your words reflect. Amplify what you are intending.

4. Believe.

If you doubt what you are saying, use it to discover why you question your intentions' validity. Focus on overcoming that resistance. Then, renew your trust in yourself. Remember that your creative powers are more potent than any uncertainty you may have. You are training your mind. To do so, you may need to become aware of some doubts before moving past them into a more actualized orientation of personal power.

5. Repeat regularly and often.

This reminds you of your destination. Affirmations can be made as a quick mind lift while you run your dog, brush your teeth, or are on hold while on the telephone. You name it—any moment you can direct your thoughts to align with your best intentions is doable. You can direct your mind to positive self-talk whenever you think of it. When reality seems to contradict your intentions, this is the time to focus your mind on a statement of your purpose with strength and confidence.

General Life-Affirming Statements

Remember to affirm using your realistic but lofty goals. These statements act as verbal and mental roadmaps to your personally chosen direction. They embody your intentions and focus. Write them on paper and leave them around your desk, car, and home to remind you of your intentions.

The following example affirmations follow the above guidelines. Some are short and catchy; others are longer and more detailed. They are grouped into statements that deal with the body, the emotions, the intellect, and the spirit. Some will feel more right for you than others. Begin with the ones that fit your intentions, and then, when you feel more confident, make up some of your own. They are quick and fun to do.

How positive and ideal can you make your mind?

Health development
- I like feeling strong and centered.
- I am filled with health and vitality. I feel great!
- My body, mind, and spirit are balanced and aligned. So this is what it feels like!
- I am relaxing inside and out.
- Relax! Enjoy living.
- Good for me. I am eating right.
- I feel strong and centered.

Intellectual confirmation
- I learn quickly and easily. Hey, I am smart.
- I am a creative thinker. What an imagination I have!
- I think clearly and grasp new ideas quickly.

- I grasp new information quickly and respond appropriately.
- I welcome the wisdom that comes to me at perfect times.
- I am flexible and creative in my thinking. I have unexpected creative flashes of thought that are strokes of genius. Amazing.
- I can see the larger patterns along with the more minor details.
- I am of unlimited potential. More of my potential opens to me each day.

Emotional stability
- I can forgive others.
- I feel full of life today.
- Today, I am focusing on the well-being of others.
- I focus on forgiving any injuries and transgressions in my life.
- I remain calm and flexible to my challenges.
- I feel relaxed, emotionally balanced, and at peace.
- I am becoming an attentive listener to my emotions and feelings.
- More and more, I respond to others and myself with loving compassion.
- I am calm and peaceful at this moment.
- I love life and am grateful for this day, relationship, home, job, sport [you name the subject that applies to your life].

Spiritual awareness
- I feel a sense of compassion for all I meet today.
- I am a trusting, loving, and loved person.
- I center myself on thoughts of peace and inspiration.
- I am connected mysteriously to all of life.
- I am fulfilling my life's purpose.
- God is guiding me. I know everything I need to know at just the right time.

Anchoring

I want to remind you about anchoring your words and feelings through your tactile and kinesthetic senses. Combining a physical movement or touch with whatever you wish to remember triggers the mind and body to work together. Neurolinguistics first introduced the importance of anchoring with a movement as an additional way to register the input when experiencing a particular moment of success.

Make up your unique movements: finger snapping, a little jig, or quieter anchoring techniques such as thoughtfully touching your finger to your chin or index fingers together. The point is to anchor yourself securely in the intention of growth.

Positive expectation leads to positive belief.

It takes discipline to consciously choose which words you will speak to yourself to expand your long-held beliefs. It takes discipline and acts of focused will to include more successful perceptions of yourself and whatever challenges you face. If you repeat, "Creative solutions come to me when I need them," three or four times a week, your self-view will expand. You will see that you often come up with creative solutions, whereas before, you saw none.

One man in a business seminar wanted to gain confidence as a creative problem solver. He began consciously noting all the problems and challenges he encountered during his days and started repeating to himself, "I am a creative problem solver."

As he became aware of his several moments of success, to his surprise, he saw that he was, in fact, an imaginative and intuitive problem solver. At a later seminar meeting, he reported that he had just realized how swiftly and effectively he handled most of his challenges. With this new realization, he changed his self-perception and stopped raking himself over the coals for problems he could not solve immediately. He changed his self-definition and upped his self-esteem.

In summary, affirmations are clearly worded statements of our desired goals. They are declarations of intention, possibility, and trust. They offer clear self-direction. Use the power of words combined with images plus feelings—and anchored with a physical reminder—to convey to yourself the clarity of your intentions and, very importantly, that what you want is possible.

A Word-Powered Exercise

You did this exercise in Chapter Ten ("A Mind Fitness Exercise: Your Life Goals/An Ideal"); now do it again. The first time, you visualized your idea; now, you will affirm your ideal.

First, write a statement about how you will be feeling as you focus on creating your "ideal" life. This is a written power symbol of your direction and intention. Here are a few ideas to help you get started.

My life is ideal when:

- I have more energy. I feel an inner sense of peace that touches all my life's actions.
- I am giving of myself in a balanced and supportive way.
- I am trusting in my relationships.
- I am doing my work to the best of my abilities.
- I have a good laugh with my coworker.
- I take time to connect with my inner quietness.
- I feel confident.

It need not be a complex statement. Be simple. Be clear. The important thing is that your statement has deep meaning in your life. Close your eyes and recreate a moment you have experienced from memory. Use that as your model. Deeply feel the emotions of the experience. Anchor that specific feeling of fulfillment and peace in your body and mind.

Choose one area where you want to experience personal recovery or expansion. It can be a situation at work, relationships, health, or an activity you want to perform more optimally. Follow the five guidelines.

Articulation of your intentions should be:

- Worded in the first-person, present tense.
- Stated clearly and positively.
- Backed by positive feelings and emotions.
- Believed it is possible.
- Repeated regularly and often.

Write your statement on a card you place on your desk, refrigerator door, mirror, or car. Please commit to repeating your intention to yourself daily with feeling and optimism.

Keep an ongoing list of the things for which you are grateful. This list of bonuses or joys will help trigger your personal expansion and affirmation.

Chapter 15

Thinking Expansively— Being Proactive on Your Own Behalf

*"To be illuminated by the steady radiance,
renewed daily, of a wonder."*
~Dag Hammarskjöld

Characteristics of Performers

WHETHER ATHLETES, ARTISTS, or business leaders, great performers have several outstanding characteristics in common: commitment, discipline, passion, vision, perseverance, confidence, creativity, and willpower. I used to wonder about their underlying thinking processes—the steps these remarkable people took to reach their optimal performances. How did they think, other than being committed and positive? What concrete change did they make in their minds to achieve their success?

I started investigating various approaches to peak performance in sports, business, education, and health, looking for commonalities. I found that all the approaches teach optimal performers to focus their minds on the still, centered space we now call mindfulness and, from this quiet, aware place, imagine experiences of success and potential.

Performers are taught to:

- Stop to be consciously quiet and focus their attention on their breathing and the center place.
- Look inward, using their senses to create their goal emotionally.
- Listen/speak directed words with a clear intention to succeed.

These three steps translate into an expanded mode of thinking that trains their intuitive intelligence and visual thinking abilities. These steps are parts of proactive reflection—the essence of Mind Fitness—practicing expanded thinking for greater creativity and health.

Champions

In recent decades, champion athletes have been making previously unheard-of breakthroughs in physical performance through "mental training." Great athletes these days have one thing in common: they speak of consciously using the power of their minds to achieve their outstanding athletic feats. They each included daily mental focus as an important part of their training regimen.

This form of mental training was initially known as mental rehearsal. First popularized in the Soviet Union and European countries, it was brought to the West through the Olympic Games and by individuals such as Austrian bodybuilder Arnold Schwarzenegger. Schwarzenegger, now better known for his action-packed films and as California Governor, was one of the first to popularize the conscious use of his mind for much of his physical success. He said, "One rep[etition] using my mind is worth twenty without."

> *The practice of seeing, feeling, and living success*
> *before it happens is a key training skill for athletes.*

Both research and the down-to-earth, real-life evidence on the playing field show the powerful connections between the mind and the body's performance. Our attitudes influence our results. If what we think and do are intimately connected, why not actively and consciously train our thoughts and expand our attitudes? We increasingly recognize that conscious self-direction leads to more explicit actions and greater personal confidence. Positive personal thinking habits form an essential foundation for overall success.

Physical Fitness to Mind Fitness

Only in the early 1960s did we as a society begin to focus on the importance of physical fitness in relation to personal health. President John Kennedy initially spoke out strongly in favor of increasing the overall physical fitness of the nation with the National Fitness Training Program.

Sixty-plus years later, the benefits of regular exercise and a low-fat diet are accepted as natural truths. We feel better physically and mentally when exercising regularly and participating in nutrition programs. We live longer when we exercise physically. The next logical step is the care and upkeep of our minds and attitudes.

Today, many of us focus on caring for and developing our minds, emotions, spirits, and bodies simply because this makes us feel and perform better daily. We are learning that some form of stress-reduction practice is as essential to our health and well-being as physical exercise. Our health increases, and our ailments lessen as we use our minds to support our bodies' mechanisms.

This new trend toward deliberate Mind Fitness programs is encouraging, but what does all this mean to you? How can it help you personally?

Mind Lifts in Action

Frank was an executive of a large manufacturing company. He knew he was prone to absorbing other people's stresses along with his own. When he was candid with himself, he knew that much of the time, he was far more anxious than he had to be. He was sensitive and reactive, becoming irritable and aggressive too quickly over minor incidents. He was excessively judgmental. He felt frustrated when things became difficult, unable to persevere through tough times and keep his sense of balance.

Frank wanted to change the way he handled stress. He needed some personalized techniques he could use to hold his center when things began to feel out of control. He explained:

"I am aware that I feel pressured and put upon. I keep trying to separate my emotional nature so I don't overreact so often at work. But then I come across as cold and zombie-like. Sometimes, I want to hit someone. I think of everything I should do, and I am continuously racing in my mind. I want to get off this treadmill of what feels like inner insanity. I realize this office is always in a crisis, so it will never improve out there. I have to change myself if I am going to prosper in this job."

One of his Mind Fitness program goals was to increase his ability to "roll with the punches" and "remain calm" when the going got rough. He began with a straightforward set of mental training techniques to achieve this new sense of resiliency. He took ten minutes each night to sit, close his eyes, and breathe. He began to center himself, increasing his awareness of his physical and emotional feelings.

He said of this first mental practice, "I remembered who I was on a deeper level and felt calm for those few minutes. Little things began to come back into perspective for me."

The other mental practice he incorporated into his daily life was verbal affirmation. He clearly and consciously set his intention. He would focus on saying carefully, five times as he stood in the shower, "I can feel calm no matter what is going on around me." He would imagine walking calmly across a green golf course during a swirling windstorm.

Whenever confronted with a challenging situation during the day, Frank would do a mind lift—that quick "pumping" of his positive statement and image—to assist himself. If he were in a hurry, he would shorten it to "I feel calm."

During his ten-minute reflection time at night, he took a deep breath, anchoring his affirmation to a calm feeling within his body. He would again imagine himself standing calmly amid a whirling storm. Frank also focused on taking three to five minutes at lunch to close his eyes and breathe, centering himself just as he did at night.

As simple and fast as these activities seem, they had an immediate impact. Within a few days, he reported feeling more self-directed and centered at work, even when the environment around him became highly demanding. His behavior toward his fellow workers became less reactive. He felt less judgmental, noticeably less tense and anxious, and more in control of his life. He transformed his thinking and automatic self-talk by consciously setting his inner direction.

Fast and Practical

For the first time, Frank felt as if he was actively directing and educating his mind. He was focusing his attitude and attention. He no longer allowed outside events to push and shove him, determining his actions and feelings. While taking conscious control of his life, he was also surrendering to it in a new way. He perceived larger patterns in his series of momentary frustrations. Frank was learning to think from the inside out rather than reacting to what was coming at him from the outside.

He got his work done, increased his productivity, and worried less about the seemingly endless demands on his time. His personal mind lifts also gave him a way to steady himself under pressure instead of just flying off the handle. Frank was gaining control of his stress level, stretching his attitudinal muscles, and giving himself an anchor. He discovered a strong link between attitude development, satisfaction, and performance.

*The key to Frank's success was quieting down long enough
to proactively shift his thinking inward toward his goals, allowing
his desired control and intuition to be activated.*

Years ago, I worked with nursing homes as a speech therapist and spoke with some wonderfully wise people with longer visions of the past than mine. An elderly lady gave some perspective on this shift of thinking when she said:

"Back before all this continuous running around, we had more time just quietly to think. People would think while walking to town, kneading bread, or tending a fire. There wasn't always a television or radio going, and we weren't always hopping in the car to drive somewhere. In my imagination, I would picture all sorts of things and pretend I was doing exactly what I wanted. I never thought of these peaceful times as mental health exercises, but that's exactly what they were. In these quiet times, I'd think and feed my mind with imaginative stories and ideas. Nowadays, we don't get much of that quiet time, making people tense and crazy."

Chapter 16

Modern Illness—Stress

"At night our fear is strong....but in the morning,
in the light, we find our courage."
~Malala Yousafze

W E ALL RECOGNIZE that there is such a tremendous growth of illnesses related to stress. We have added cell phones, text/e-mails, and social media to the information overload in our lives. No wonder as stress mounts, people feel out of control and helpless. We all know that feeling. "Help, I'm frantic; I can't do it all!" Or, in defeat, "What's the use, anyway?" We feel both overwhelmed and helpless to change the situation.

The new-old news is that constant distractions create inner stress, which wears down the immune system, allowing viruses and runaway cells to gain a foothold within the body. Stress takes its toll on both the body and mind. Stress affects people differently, but medicine is unraveling a common thread connecting illness to an individual's ability to cope with life's demands and pressures.

Fortunately, we are also learning something new from behavioral medicine. Biofeedback, mindfulness meditation, yoga, walking, especially in nature, and other stress-reduction methods have demonstrated strong relationships between mind and body, especially in cardiology and immune functioning. At Stanford University and Harvard Medical School, researchers have shown conclusively that people can safely influence physiological functions such as blood flow, heart rate, body temperature, and hormonal secretions through such techniques as mental imagery, relaxation, meditation, visualization, and active suggestion. These techniques have proven effective in reducing stress, treating cancer, easing childbirth, managing pain in burn clinics, and maintaining overall physical health.

Deficiencies

We all understand what fitness and its opposite, deficiency, mean. Suppose we do not take care of our bodies with food and exercise. In that case, we may experience a wide range of symptoms related to those deficiencies, reflecting our physical, mental, or spiritual malnutrition.

- Physical symptoms include reduced immunity, lack of muscle tone, anemia of different kinds, osteoporosis, chronic tiredness, a higher risk of heart disease, poor circulation, and other disorders.
- Mental symptoms include depression, poor concentration, psychological distortion, and addictions, resulting in self-abusive behaviors and low self-esteem with a diminished ability to translate ideas or dreams into effective, real-world actions.
- Spiritual deficiencies result in alienation in which one cannot perceive oneself as part of a larger whole. This personal isolation results in loneliness, narrowing the capacity for relating, compassion, caring, and love.

Just as our bodies need proper nutrition and care to achieve optimum health, our minds and spirits must be cared for and nurtured. We can accomplish the former by changing our diets (for example, eating fewer fats and refined carbohydrates) and running or walking a few miles daily. We can achieve the latter by regularly feeding and exercising our minds with quiet, imaginative ideas and positive attitudes.

Like our muscles, our spirit, mind, and attitude can be strengthened for greater stamina, responsiveness, and resiliency.

Being Proactive: Personal Development

Dr. Gerald Jampolsky, a pioneer in attitudinal and spiritual psychology, writes, "The mind can be retrained. Within this fact lies our freedom. No matter how often we have misused it, the mind can be utilized in a way that is so positive that, at first, it is beyond anything we can imagine."

Personal development is nothing mysterious. It requires simply allowing time and attention to get to know yourself in a fuller and purposeful way. This increases your ability to participate in directing your life in three essential ways.

1. You give yourself time to reflect and think.
2. You have more clarity about your life's essential things and purposes. Fostering your intuitive intelligence helps you clarify your values for the life contributions you want to make.
3. You are doing something to concretely aim your thoughts, attitudes, and actions in the direction you want to take.

One man said, "I am gaining the strength to pursue my dream, to break it down one day at a time, and make it real for myself. Before now, I felt like my life was one long aerobics class. Now I feel more like I'm in an art class." He is no longer a victim of circumstances. He is moving from barely handling daily life to creating a life of full potential for himself. Such a person is on the road to becoming healthy and robust within, no matter the outer circumstances of his life.

Get in touch with your inner strength, humor, wisdom, and yes, gratitude, and you will develop the integrating power of your intuitive intelligence and the Divine Spirit. This is not a cure-all, but you will begin to experience positive changes and new insights in many areas of your life. Be willing to play a self-determined part in moving toward your fullest potential on all levels of your being. Encourage yourself by actively training your mental and spiritual capacities to perceive fuller, subtler patterns while developing a sense of hardiness in your reactions.

Mind Fitness is an attitude and a set of tools
for optimal health and personal empowerment.

Antidotes: Stress Focusing Exercise

In Chapter Four, you were asked to identify your stresses. In this exercise, pick just one of them to focus on. There may be several you want to focus on simultaneously, but for the point of this exercise, identify one evident stress that pulls you to a place of "insanity."

Create a mental picture of what you could do to balance that stress. This mental picture becomes one of your stress-relieving tools—your "mental antidote."

For example, if your stress comes from feeling tired and nervous, your antidote might be focusing on inner peace and relaxation. For that, you could imagine yourself sitting in a beach chair, soothed by the rhythmic sound of the waves and the salty tang of the air.

If your stress comes from ill health, your antidote may be to feel strong and healthy. For that, you might imagine yourself walking up a hill in the beauty of nature.

If your stress comes from a stressful relationship, the antidote might be to imagine laughing with the other person comfortably over the dinner table. Perhaps your response is, "Oh, I could never laugh with that person and feel good." Remember, you are stretching and expanding your mental possibilities. Don't pressure yourself to create this scene first in real life. *Imagine* it first as your antidote to the stress. You may be amazed at how soon it can happen.

To expand your mental possibilities, imagine your ideal antidotes to your identified stress in the present in as vivid a sensory detail as possible. Feel as enthusiastic as you can about what you're visualizing.

Now, encourage yourself to expand your thinking further by affirming in words, with conviction and passion, "I am creating this new thought in my life now" or " I am doing this now."

Chapter 17

Empowered

"There is only one kind of love,
but thousands of different versions."
~La Rochefoucauld, 1650

The Empowered Individual

EMPOWERMENT FOCUSES YOUR energy on contributing optimally to your own life's fulfillment. It is thinking of yourself with optimism and love. It is living your unique life path and gifts in a developed way. Empowerment comes from being an individual who is a part of the greater whole. It embodies the energies of self-reliance, integrity, and interconnection. With empowerment, self-determination, intuitive intelligence, and even what is called divine wisdom meet in harmony.

Empowerment comes through your own choices. You have free will and realize no one else can do it for you. You give yourself the ultimate gift of intuition, confidence, and trust. You can be encouraged by others, but in the end, you must do it for and to yourself. Each of us must be our own source of belief and choice.

This is an excellent time to develop a "road map" for your journey toward full potential and empowerment. From this description, you can visualize what your personal empowerment feels like.

Use this expansion on the characteristics of empowered people, first described in Chapter Three, to help stimulate your thinking.

Empowered People

- They are creative and open to life, demonstrating a sense of possibility, direction, and general affirmation of life. They can suspend right/wrong judgments and think of many options.
- They are grounded and realistic in their choice of actions. Failure or risk does not stop them.
- They make their own decisions. They are willing to move out of the safe space of "That can't be done" or "I don't know" to the more responsible and empowered place of "Here's what I am going to try..."
- They feel strong enough to take action on their own behalf. They have enough discipline and will to act to take steps to move forward in the direction of their vision.
- They have a sense of union with all of life—you might call it a spiritual relationship. They have a strong sense of self-esteem. They know what they can do and understand their strengths and weaker points. As a result, they are less fearful, and others perceive them to be generally loving and supportive.

Is this a high standard to live up to? Indeed it is. Please understand that empowered people aren't perfect, nor do they feel perfect. Don't expect perfection from yourself. Impossible goals undermine the empowerment process. It is self-defeating to expect to feel great in every aspect of your life all the time. But you will begin to have more feelings of balance than before. These characteristics naturally grow within you as you progress toward a sense of flow in your personal empowerment.

Belief + Will + Skills = Empowered Actions

The winning formula for empowerment is:

- The belief is that your life direction comes from you and that your goals are possible.
- The will and discipline to persevere through difficult times.
- The mental, emotional, and physical skills needed to generate your desired quality of life.

Self-empowerment is active; it involves physical confidence in your ability with the help of luck and whatever higher power you may connect with. It can be summed up as "I'll do my best."

Empowerment is the belief that you will do your best to meet life's challenges whenever they occur.

1. Belief in self.

High self-esteem is belief in yourself—confidence in your learning and expanding ability. You affirm in the words "I can do it!" or "It can be done!" or "Let's give it a try!"—whether to handle stress, overcome an unwanted life pattern, or attain a sought-after goal.

It is the firm belief that your chosen life goals are attainable.

2. The will to take action.

More demanding tasks call for the will to take action. The will to take action means having the energy, discipline, and perseverance to do whatever it takes to bring possibility into form. This can be the hardest part. To learn the new skills that empowered action demands, you often need to push yourself intensely to persevere through the inevitable mistakes that lead to new learning. Being a student is a case in point. Most students must study hard to meet the demands and skills to accomplish their goals.

Nothing squashes self-empowerment and self-esteem faster than setting your expectations too high. Most of us are willing to expend some energy for true success. If you ask too much of yourself, you may quit. Create attainable steps. I like to succeed, so I try to set reasonable, "do-able" self-expectations. Sometimes, you *must* push yourself when it is just plain more challenging than expected. These are the moments when your will, self-discipline, and perseverance get tested.

3. The needed skills.

Reaching any goal will require know-how: the skills and knowledge needed to do the job. When you take a risk, you want a reasonable expectation of success and a good safety net beneath you. This doesn't mean you must know all the answers or possess all the skills initially.

Instead, it means you have a good solid bank of life skills and the confidence you can learn as you go along and the situation demands. One of the most essential skills is the sense that you can usually figure out the solutions to life's problems and job requirements.

***Aim for the empowerment skill of naturally
doing what needs to be done at the right time.***

Chapter 18

Dynamic Love

The essence of empowerment is dynamic love.

In CHAPTER ONE, I said that empowered sanity lives with an attitude of dynamic love. With that loving attitude of optimism comes a more profound peace, explicit purpose, and gentler compassion. What a superb goal to have in life…to live in dynamic love. Active, outreaching, and responding to the moment. It is the energy within empowerment: having confidence in your ability to handle your life situations from a home base of love for yourself and your abilities. That doesn't mean you have it all the time, but *most* of the time. It is your clear intention and direction. Dynamic love is the present-oriented power behind your balancing act, bringing your emotions and feelings into a deep sense of action-oriented optimism.

Living with an attitude of dynamic love is an
optimistic, fluid, creatively engaged way to live free from fear.

Feelings don't often fit neatly into words, but we have all experienced dynamic love when we have seen the best in ourselves or someone else. We see dynamic love when you reach out to another, saying, "Yes, I am with you." It is an adaptable energy; its first response is active compassion and kindness. It is the aspiration to evoke the best. All these are the natural responses of a mature and emotionally aligned person. Only fear, in one of its many forms, makes us respond in ways other than with love.

Empowered people tend to have deep connections with others and experience love not only for the people with whom they come in contact but also for all of life. Such dynamic love lives in the mind relatively free from fear and self-doubts. You orient yourself towards being as expansive and supportive of yourself and others as possible. You express yourself with constructive and compassionate thoughts and actions.

The energy from this love is alive with expression and promotes actions of integrity and open potential. Possibilities open up with the expansion of "I can't" or "it won't work" limitations. Optimism is the key attitude shift here. We all know the difference between living or working with someone fearful and negative or someone confident and creative—one lives in pessimism, and the other in optimistic and enlivening dynamic love.

> ***Dynamic love is not a phrase relegated to the***
> ***narrow realms of romance but a creatively***
> ***expansive, optimistic, and fully alive way of living.***

Such love comes alive as present moments are lived in an expansive way of thinking; it allows confidence and risk-taking. It is proactive. It recognizes more significant, often unseen patterns that interrelate with each other. Such optimistic energy is rooted in the belief that collective human consciousness develops as we individually grow. Love is more than compassion. It expresses deep positive faith that all life forms are interrelated. An evolution in personal thinking expands our human, social, and global potential with our empowerment.

Vesti's Story

A long-time family friend and my childhood art mentor, Vesti, fit the portrait of dynamic love. What a life she had! A wonder to others, she lived her life faithful to her inner self. She was born in St. Petersburg, Russia, at the turn of the century. During the 1917 Russian Revolution, her family fled to China, where she spent her adolescent years. As a young adult, she lived in Berlin, moving to London right before World War II. She moved to Greenwich Village in New York, where she lived until the mid-eighties. That is where she came into my early life. Each time she moved, she embarked on a new career.

At 67, she moved a final time to Venice, saying, "I will study the mosaics of the masters." The pursuit of beauty was the constant inner truth that ran through all of her life's work. It was her artistry in life.

Vesti never had much money, but she was genuinely prosperous. Her zest for life was magnetic, and everyone loved her. She was wise, entertaining, and genuine. In her home, you met the taxi driver and the ambassador. Class, age, and nationality meant nothing to her. Each person she met was a treasure to be delighted in and shared with others. Each found their commonality through her great human spirit.

She developed her artistic skills over the years and intended to produce her highly esteemed ceramic and mosaic work. She often worked all hours of the night because she said, "I love it; I can't imagine my life without my work. What would I do?" She used to laugh and say that she was illiterate in seven languages, but no one was better at telling stories and jokes in every accent and dialect imaginable.

Vesti was an empowered person. She faced more change, loneliness, and hardships than most of us do, yet she always had hope in tomorrow and joy in today. She shared her sadness and her joys openly, without fear of embarrassment. She loved life and people. Her work and play overlapped as she created her art. Time flew, and she thrived in the present moment. She is my model of dynamic love in action.

Can you think of someone who is your real-life role model?

Who is the Vesti in your life?

What are the characteristics of this individual you admire?

Consciously Designing Your Life

Now may be the time for you to have the courage to believe in the best of your potential. You can use the untapped power of the imaginative mind to become influential on your own behalf—creating love, inner peace, self-expression, and skilled accomplishment—and to increase your overall health and fulfillment in life. As you actively develop new mental habits and become aware of your present moments contributing to a sense of purpose, you discover more joy, optimism, success, and, yes, less stress.

You choose a life about self-determination and possibilities rather than limitations and barriers. You feel yourself actively becoming a creative force, working toward your balance in a heartfelt and committed way. One joy leads to another, and one growth step to another. This is the essence of thriving in a mindset of dynamic love.

It takes courage and commitment to exercise anything, including your imaginative thinking. It is a choice to regularly practice being aware of your present moments while aiming your intentions and internal dialogue in expanded thoughts and ideal visions. As you concentrate on developing this kind of awareness and optimism within yourself, you naturally identify and outgrow fears that may have consciously or unconsciously limited you for years. Shadows vanish in the light. Restrictions dissipate. You learn attitudes and actions that encompass deeper values and ideals.

> **Being a dynamically loving person is**
> **a skill to be cultivated and nurtured.**

Intentions Reshaping Your Life

Because we are human and subject to pain, fear, and anger, we cannot assume that love will just come to us without being called. We must make known our intention to give love—first and foremost to ourselves—and then do something about it.

As you become proactive about self-growth and awareness, you focus on love and health as something you consciously create. Then, the healing process begins. Fear and anger start to dissolve, controlling you less as you recognize and choose to confront them. As you focus on moment-to-moment living, you proactively learn to love.

> **Loving and believing in yourself are**
> **at the very heart of personal growth.**

By adopting an inner awareness of reshaping your life, you have given yourself a gift of kindness and power. As you place your spiritual essence at the center of your life, you begin to sense your connection to all of life and with something infinite—some indefinable spirit that allows us to go beyond where we were into a greater possibility. By committing to a daily time of quiet introspection, you begin a life with increased awareness, guiding you to move consciously out of your long-standing habits and attitudes. In its place, an expressive, skillful life emerges, built on a more significant articulation of your values and what is important to you. A new, intuitively felt pattern becomes apparent. You experience, on a deeper level, the unlimited capacity to be whatever you know is right for you, with fewer imposed boundaries or limits. Empowerment is living your highest ideals and visionary thoughts—or, at minimum, aiming in that direction. It becomes a life goal and a place to return to during confusion and difficulty in your life.

Initially, you will focus your mental exercise sessions on external activities: improving your running or weightlifting, or in professional areas, such as changing careers, being a better manager, or simply getting to work on time. You may want to concentrate on being a receptive student to master a new area of interest, improve your health, or be a better parent, spouse, or friend.

As your practice develops, you can start by acknowledging the characteristics that please you before moving on to the personal characteristics you wish to develop more fully within yourself. This expansion comes with increased awareness of your directions and choices. As you reflect quietly, focus on how it feels, looks, and sounds to be patient, articulate, self-assured, soft-spoken, assertive, or whatever other qualities you may want to embrace. Imagine as many different desired characteristics as you can. You are engaging in positive mind play. Make it fun for yourself. Supportive personal characteristics will begin to grow within you as you allow yourself to label and focus quietly on them. Give yourself that personal road map.

Developing your inner self will color all your experiences and perceptions. Optimizing one area of your life always spills over into all other areas. This rich, creative thinking applies just as well in corporate settings as in the learning, health, and personal relationship worlds. You may move beyond the physical and psychological realm into the spiritual realm. This is a realm of mystery with its intuition, creativity, and connection to the unknown infinite. In this larger pattern, optimism and love are the basis from which personal self-esteem and compassion radiate.

Love results from healthy human functioning;
we feel it naturally when we are in balance
with each other and ourselves.

An Empowering Exercise

1. Close your eyes and take a few deep breaths as you "Stop." Focus on inward sensations as you mentally open your intuition. Opening to your intuition entails quieting the outside world and allowing new patterns and insights to come to mind.

    - Ask yourself how you would feel if your survival needs were met. What kind of home, financial savings, food, and transportation would you have?

    - Now take a few minutes and imagine yourself surrounded by all your physical survival needs. Use your growing visual thinking skills and think descriptively. Write down your thoughts.

2. What would you need to feel at peace with your emotional and psychological needs? What kinds of support and respect do you need from your family, friends, and work partners? Imagine knowing that you are psychologically safe.

3. Ask yourself what you would need to express your creative side. Imagine yourself living your creative passion. Allow those feelings to wash over you as you begin to understand what you would ideally like to do as you learn to live a satisfying and empowering life. Stay open to new insights from your expanding intuitive intelligence.

4. Now, replace all of these goals with just one goal: expressing your dynamic love in whatever form or forms it may take for you. Create a deep appreciation and respect for yourself, your family, your relationships, your community, and your planet in your inner mind.

5. Feel a sense of unlimited possibilities as you expand your thinking beyond judgments, imagining only the most optimal possibilities. Allow that soothing feeling of dynamic love to surround you as your single purpose for just a few moments.

This is the destination.

Chapter 19

Become What You Image

*"The mind is a strange machine which can combine
the materials offered to it in the most astonishing ways."*
~Bertrand Russell

Self-Fulfilling Prophecy

ATHLETES BEGIN THEIR training in mind power early. In my youth, I trained to be a competitive swimmer. I remember using mental training techniques naturally without knowing what I was doing. As I swam, moving my arms and legs in rhythm, I counted to four as I saw, felt, and heard each stroke in my mind. Soon, I became the movement I perceived in my mind's eye. I felt my senses come into balance as I raced through the water.

After practice, as I lay relaxing in the sun, I relived the experience of swimming with ease, power, and grace. In my imagination, my thoughts were unconstrained; I swam to my full potential. In my vision, I believed totally in my abilities. At first, the "perfect" swims I experienced in my mind were only daydreams that my mind created naturally. But over time, those dreams became manifest in the physical world as actual swims that were as close to perfection as I could dream. I instinctively knew there was a connection between my thoughts and feelings and how well I performed physically. Only years later would I understand the connection.

Recent research shows that thoughts are packed with information affecting our physical health and ability to meet challenges. Put in down-to-earth terms, if you think you will fail, you usually do fail. Hopeless, negative thinking leads to ineffective, adverse action. Dr. Willis Harman, past president of the Institute of Noetic Sciences, states:

"One of the most far-reaching findings related to consciousness has been dubbed the 'self-fulfilling prophecy.' Our conscious and unconscious beliefs create the future in ways more subtle and powerful than we ordinarily consider."

Mind Bridge

Through regular mental training, you focus on learning how to use your mind as a bridge between your inner knowing—your values, intuition, and spiritual self—and your capacity to act in the world. You incorporate core, whole-brain thinking skills that you can apply to any endeavor.

Daily reflection is a personal commitment to engage in self-education at the most intimate level—within your own mind.
Steven wanted to play the drums but never seemed to find the time or energy to sit down and play. He always seemed to find important things to do that got in the way. Steven talked a lot about his desire, but his commitment to himself needed to be there. He had yet to prioritize music, and this stalemate remained a frustrating desire for years.

Steven realized that his commitment to himself needed to be up-leveled when he began to do some self-development work. He needed to open his mind to accept doing something that would be an intimate act of self-love. It became clear that playing the drums was something he would be doing just for himself, not for anyone else. There were no outside gains for him to make, only personal joy and pleasure. Could he give himself that permission?

He began his personalized program toward well-being by taking a few minutes daily to visualize himself drumming. He concentrated on feeling and seeing his hands move in rhythm. More importantly, he visualized himself accepting the fun and deep satisfaction he would gain by adding music to his life. He took some time to let his intuitive sense come up with the words, "I care enough about myself to play the drums."

After about a month of mental focusing, Steven made time to begin group lessons—a sign of personal growth on an intense and meaningful level. His commitment to himself began to take on an external form as he translated his desire into action. Although he has not become a professional rock band drummer, Steven now feels a new sense of power and fun as he plays music with others and for himself. He said, "I laugh much more at myself and the fun of doing something I have always wanted to do." He added more seriously, "I have learned to love and respect myself profoundly and deeply by learning to listen and play rhythms."

That, very simply, is the feeling of being a hero in your own life…doing something not for outside recognition but for a fuller sense of self.

How Long?

The first question is often, "How long should I quiet myself?" Although it's a plus to spend *any* brief time slowing yourself down to notice your attitudes, thoughts, and beliefs while consciously setting your direction, most people who work up to twenty minutes find it effective for optimal fitness. That gives them time to get involved in their inner world without losing focus.

> *Stay aware of your personal rhythm.*
> *You are your judge.*
> *The goal is to create time each day*
> *to engage in the practice of inner quiet.*

Some people love ten minutes in the morning and ten at night. Others take two-minute periods throughout the day, working up to longer stretches when they can. I recommend quieting yourself for ten to twenty minutes three or four times a week for a beginning maintenance mental fitness workout. Begin with short warm-up stretch movements and end with a self-acknowledgment. This way, it becomes a part of your lifestyle, not something special you add occasionally. Mental, emotional, and spiritual self-care are innovations in your thinking that you want to make part of your life, as integrated as the care of your body, home, family, and, of course, your pets.

***It takes a courageous and self-caring
attitude to start taking yourself seriously.***

Remember to:
- Create time for your inner quiet.
- Quiet yourself.
- Use your quiet time to focus your awareness, using your breath as your anchor.
- When quiet, allow yourself to stop, reflect, and expand your thinking.

This new attitude of self-care is not selfishness but rather a commitment to caring for yourself in the same way you care for someone in your family. You want to do what is best for that person. You wish them well and want to see them grow to be as healthy and happy as possible. As you start actively applying those feelings of positive regard toward yourself, you expand your potential for those experiences.

Beliefs and attitudes are usually lifelong habits. You may have spent years believing you could only be a certain way.

***Use your mental focusing abilities
to expand limited thinking habits.***

Inner mind exercising means reversing long-held beliefs and proactively establishing new ones. Generating and developing new thought patterns takes time and attention, especially initially. It takes focus and a disciplined will to quiet yourself daily. Mind Fitness takes concentration, but you will be delighted and surprised at how much benefit and pleasure you derive from it.

Starting your practice is a decisive vote of renewed confidence in yourself and your future. It represents your commitment to honoring the creative potential within yourself, others, and the life around you. It is a shift in thinking that affects all aspects of your life.

Taking Time Out

An essential part of Mind Fitness is taking time out *regularly* to care for your mental state in the same way you may be taking time to care for your body. Without regular exercise, certain parts of your mind and spirit are inclined to atrophy negatively, just as your muscles atrophy when not used. To put some muscle into your attitude, you want to "pump images" like you might "pump iron." You build mental hardiness muscles that help you de-stress and focus on your ideal attitudes and actions.

> *Engage in conscious quieting,*
> *followed by active flexing of your*
> *highest intentions and attitudinal muscles.*

For some people, these are prayer sessions; for others, meditation and contemplation or active imaging and focusing. They are gifts you give yourself—you decide how best to spend a few moments of focused time. These special times are yours alone, allowing you to deepen your relationship with yourself. Such time-out contemplation provides a few minutes to balance your body, mind, and spirit.

Rob stated his need for time out: "When I get stressed, everything in my life looks terrible. I get depressed and scattered. Everything is overwhelming, and, worst of all, I am full of overreactions and self-pity." In a nutshell, stress produces negative attitudes and reactions.

My Story: An Attitude Change

When I started working in schools as a speech pathologist, I was assigned to classrooms of severely handicapped students. The students were functioning far below age level, most with no speech or, at best, a few hard-to-understand words. They were hyperactive; some had autistic symptoms; all were challenging to work with.

I spent the first few weeks in despair and frustration. I felt out of control and defeated. I was feeling stressed. How was I to work productively with these young people? How could I contribute to their communication?

My internal dialogue repeated, "I can't do this," and "I don't want to be doing this." My fear of inadequacy was winning out, and my attitude slid downhill. I was developing limited and creatively uninspired thinking. My work showed it, too. I needed an attitude change—and quickly. I took a day off to come to grips with the situation.

> ***If I was going to work with these exceptional youngsters,***
> ***I needed a better attitude, which took a conscious effort.***

I decided to put my mind into serious training. To begin to move from an attitude of frustration to enjoyment, I pushed myself to pump images of success using mind lifts. I worked from the premise that "I can become what I visualize" and consciously imagined a new attitude toward my job. I began to slow down long enough to focus my mental energies in the desired direction.

I pushed myself to train a new perception, to see the positives—because the negatives were too apparent. I needed to give my psyche at least a fighting chance to balance. So, I began to look for fulfilling moments.

As part of my mental training, I would stop and take five deep breaths each morning before I got out of the car. I would then *look* as I imagined and visually pictured myself enjoying the work and helping students. I *listened and spoke* as I told myself, "I will find many moments of satisfaction and humor during the day. I will help my kids learn."

I began consciously acknowledging and naming moments of learning satisfaction in my days in the classroom. I noticed student success and more humorous, fun moments. Whenever I had the slightest hint of satisfaction or shared a laugh with another person, I would say, "See, that was a moment of accomplishment and humor. Finally, I could say, "I am having more and more fun moments. Things are improving."

As my attitude improved, my skill level and intuitive knowledge of what to do with these exceptional young students developed. I began enjoying my work and naturally became more effective at the same time. I was happier, and the year ended with concrete gains in their communication abilities.

__Mind Fitness is based on powerful__
__connections between the mind and the body,__
__between attitudes and actions, and what you think and do.__

Your personalized "let's get it back in balance" training routine can shift your attitudes away from dead-end thinking. This does not instantaneously cure anything, but it gives you a direction of focus when you feel the need for some changes—to get a grip and regain your sense of sanity when needed. I learned to balance my negative thinking by acknowledging the "ups" in my day. To do so took discipline and mental focus, but it was more than worth the effort!

Lifting Your Mind and Attitude

I have talked a good deal about mind lifts as an essential tool in teaching yourself your new attitude—a means of lifting yourself to your fullest potential. Yoga instructor Shirley Dockstader created the term "mind lifts" to play off the word "pumping iron," but with this method, you lift something lighter than air—images, mental photographs. Mind lifting keeps your energy where it will most support your life goals. It is really just another term for self-talk or mind chatter that is guided and self-determined rather than randomly roaming around your mind in some often-unconscious way.

Guiding your thinking to optimize yourself means you are doing some form a mind lift several times daily as you become increasingly clear on your direction and life choices. A mind lift may be as simple as taking a deep breath while standing in line. As you exhale, imagine sitting in your favorite living room chair, relaxed and at peace. You see a mental photograph of the scene. Remember, this is self-education; you'll get better and better at designing and directing your thinking to support yourself in a happier healthier way.

This is what I did with my school job. I kept reminding myself what I wanted to experience, and then, whenever I experienced a brief moment of that feeling, I consciously acknowledged it. My attention was focused on desired character qualities such as humor, understanding, and patience. Whenever I laughed or was effective, I would say to myself, "See, this is what you want to be doing."

This experience again taught me that I could teach myself to focus on what I wanted to develop in my life instead of just allowing my mind to chatter away on the habitual negatives idly. I focused on keeping my ideals out front, which helped me turn my attitude around.

With mind lifts, you build and shape your attitudinal muscles to fit your visions. You can use them whenever you think of it. Use thoughts such as achieving your goals, appreciating your close relationships, solving problems, meeting challenges, and uplifting attitudes—the direction is unique for each of us. The important thing is to make short mind lifts come alive for you.

***Solid and healthy attitudes are like strong,
healthy muscles—they stay that way when used and exercised.***

Chapter 20

Changing Habits

"Gratitude begins in our hearts and then details into behavior.
It almost always makes you willing to be of service,
which is where the joy resides."
~Anne LaMott

Many of the limits you may be putting on yourself come from childhood and have just developed into long-term habits of thought that are now outdated. These thinking patterns were mostly learned unconsciously when we were more limited in understanding. Most of us did what we thought was needed or expected; if these behaviors worked, we adopted them as a way of life without much thought. They have become long-standing habits and coping behaviors. Decades later, you may find yourself using those same coping behaviors whether or not they are now relevant to anything in your life. They may not be leading you toward a happier, more fulfilled life. They may be limiting you.

Here's an example of how an old pattern was examined and turned around. I counseled a woman who had been working on her habit of overeating. She had turned to food all her life when depressed or under stress. This had caused her a great deal of pain. We began to use imagination drawings as a means to learn emotional literacy. She went back to the beginning of this behavior pattern, to the fourth grade when a teenage neighbor had molested her. She had not told anyone because she was ashamed and afraid. Instead, she began eating, which she now thinks was how she tried to cover up her intense feelings of shame. She said:

"I now recognize that my desire to eat strengthens whenever I feel I have done something wrong. I may never get rid of my eating desire when stressed, but at least now I know where it comes from. I am learning strategies of action that let me channel my feelings more appropriately. It is always an active choice on my part, and I know I have to make that choice each time I feel myself slipping backward. I will now sit down and quietly try to identify what is bothering me, then grab an apple or something healthy to put in my mouth as I run out the door for a walk or call a friend. More and more of the time, I win. Although it's not gone, my urge to eat does not control me so often."

People often adopt certain behaviors as a conscious or unconscious way to handle a situation that feels out of control or to blunt physical or emotional pain. The problem is that this strategy just as effectively stifles their happiness in the long run as it stifles the pain. As you become aware of the patterns within your thoughts, you can choose which are helpful today and which are not. You can begin to heal those old patterns and fears.

Psychotherapists, recovery programs, and self-development groups help people in this vital personal awareness and healing work. Many development programs have made personal growth available and affordable to all seeking direction and support. Inner mind training is about learning to be aware and mindful of your thoughts and actions, transforming those holding you back.

Evolution in Thinking

Daily mental care evolves how you think about life and yourself.
As your insights and attitudes expand, you begin to experience greater understanding and creativity, allowing you to contribute more to yourself and others. Many people who practice Mind Fitness come to feel that their life situations are occurring for the ultimate good, even if they don't fully understand them. As a result, they need not be so afraid to take risks and chances as they learn more about themselves, their spiritual nature, and how to care for both.

Key Ideas

Mind Fitness, like physical fitness, is a continual process encouraged by the practice of mind skills. Here are some thoughts that we have gathered about Mind Fitness and mental health, i.e. "sanity":

- Sanity, as in balanced mental health, is an ongoing process. We evolve by continually becoming aware of and refining the quality of our lives. We move from physical survival through emotional safety to self-actualization, which has powerful energies toward love, creativity, and relationships.

- Mind Fitness uses the known learning techniques of visual thinking and inner language as a daily practice to influence attitudes and actions.

- These practical mindful tools work as building blocks or core learning skills, making learning more accessible.

- By committing to a daily time of introspection and imagery, you begin a lifestyle of quiet awareness, consciously directing yourself.

- You exercise your intuitive intelligence and see a larger pattern to life goals.

- You experience the meaning of unlimited capacity to guide your own life on a deeper level, aiming your energies where you want them to go.

- Optimizing one area of your life always spills over into all the other areas.

- Love is genuinely our home base. The desire to contribute love and be loved is fundamental to all human beings.

- You can consciously focus on the rich attitude of dynamic love that, once started, will grow steadily in your life.

- Relationship, creativity, and health are characteristics of people who lead mentally fit, empowering lives.

From this dynamic state of mind and heart, you can better take on challenges without holding yourself back. Relationships, health, and work will become more satisfying as your practice of daily mental care and contemplation becomes a part of your life.

Exercise: Images of Happiness

The following exercise helps you name short and long-term goals.

Images of fulfilled happiness: Most people do not often consider what life would look and feel like if they were fulfilled and happy. Take a few moments now to visualize yourself as a content, fulfilled person.

- What would you be doing?
- Who would be with you?
- How would you be feeling?
- What values would you be expressing?
- What would your attitudes and outlook on life be?
- How would your life look and feel?
- Name three things that bring you happiness.

Take time to experience how you would most ideally be. Make a game of looking within to define what it would be like if *you* were happy. When you have a moment of happiness, acknowledge and label it to yourself.

Give yourself a few weeks to do this exercise. Remember to acknowledge moments of happiness by creating visual images to reinforce such moments. Keep refining and expanding them. This is a step in clarifying your directions.

Chapter 21

Creative Thinking

*"More and more, creative thinking is becoming valued
as the essential ingredient in change and in progress."*
~Edward de Bono

DURING MY COUNTRY living days in Hawaii, I saw creation alive and blooming in abundance. There was no slowing it. Everything was growing and multiplying at an astounding rate. I noted a strong contrast between early computer games and Mother Nature. With games, you would shoot to destroy in some form or another. Everything was based on making the number of these little symbols on the screen smaller to having things disappear. On the other hand, outside our window, nature was forever generative: adding on and creating new abundant things— new bananas, weeds, flowers, rain, and rainbows.

Creative thought is like that. Creative thinking generates constructive new ideas, insights, and thoughts in abundance. It uses the brain's intuitive, image-creating abilities. Creative thinking invites you to expand your mind, generating new possibilities that allow you to operate at levels previously beyond your scope.

*Creative thinking means combining the many functions
of the mind and spirit in synergistic, integrated ways
so that the whole becomes more significant than the sum of its parts.*

Intuition

Let's go deeper into intuition. Intuition is a sense or intelligence that actively synthesizes very subtle perceptions. It is the gut-level instinctive knowing that we all have felt at particular moments. Intuition is the mysterious, spiritual, unknown part of the mind. We may not be able to see or touch it, but we surely know when it is active.

The intuitive is a subtle knowing rather than a rational understanding. This kind of intelligence organizes more extraordinary patterns of perception, interrelating seemingly unrelated elements into meaningful wholes. It leads you to think in patterns and layers of association, revealing innovative realms of thought and action. From here, new vision, understanding, and possibilities take hold in the mind.

> ***Our intuitive flashes of insight lead to***
> ***making decisions of greater wisdom.***

Developing the whole brain and spirit involves dusting off that often underused part of the mind to create more options and a more comprehensive range of responses. Thinking in multi-layered wholes, rather than individual, unrelated parts, leads to a greater and more playful perspective and the ability to see new combinations and new patterns of insight.

This form of thinking is commonly referred to as instinctual because it comes from the inside rather than from the outside. It often contradicts what you had previously thought to be sound and rational, but when you dare to follow those instincts, they frequently prove to be correct in some mysterious way. With its symbols, intuition is your gateway to the unconscious, where your most powerful thoughts and urges emerge.

The intuition speaks softly but persistently in flashes of insight and awareness. Insight means just that: inner seeing. It does not scream or obsess; that is the ego's voice. Intuition is the image, the sensation, the feeling, and the spirit that comes when you sit quietly in an unstressed state, totally relaxed. It has a sense of fullness and honesty. It is another level of perception and understanding that is larger and more interconnected than normal cognition. You may see an image in your mind's eye, a mental picture pointing toward a fuller experience, a more profound wisdom. Intuition may come as a thought that keeps returning, a sound or sentence in your head, or a gut feeling running through you.

This inner wisdom is not just some ephemeral, passive sense. It goes by many names and takes many forms. Each culture and spiritual tradition has its own words for it. This wisdom acts as a conduit through which you translate ideals and life purposes into attainable goals and actions. It is our spiritual center and a part of our true nature, an essence through which we create a larger, more interconnected purpose. Through reflection, we perceive more of the whole, with all its patterns and associations.

By purposely strengthening intuitive intelligence through this kind of low-key, purposeful mental training, we gain increased clarity of thought and more self-directed daily functioning. Focusing on developing your intuitive intelligence—sometimes called the inner voice—involves learning to sense and trust a deep personal direction. Many people spend a lifetime pursuing goals that do not come from themselves, and as a result, sadly, they find little personal meaning or satisfaction in their attainments. We express ourselves more honestly and authentically as we perceive our larger pattern from inner wisdom. We see our values more clearly, we can better articulate them, and our actions are more directed and self-assured.

Intimately connected to the insights gained from your intuitive intelligence is a relationship with something more profound than your own individual humanity. You feel illuminated and renewed daily for your journey through life. Sensing your control over your life's purpose while at the same time surrendering your control to that purpose is the ultimate paradox. It is awe-inspiring to feel your potential expanding while sensing this comes from something other than your ordinary sense of yourself. We've all heard, "The whole is greater than the sum of its parts." This is possible because of the intelligence within creativity.

Intuitive intelligence—a theme throughout this book—runs akin to all forms of identified intelligence. This form of knowing perceives patterns and insights, combining and synthesizing bits and pieces of experience and abstract knowledge we never even knew we had. It brings new understanding from nowhere and from everywhere. As the athlete, mathematician, or writer needs training to develop their natural inclinations, so does the intuitive intelligence respond to awareness and training.

How intuition works is a mystery, but people are increasingly becoming consciously aware of this sixth sense. Parents often intuitively know when their children are about to walk through the door or have a sense of something wrong, even when the child is not visible. Sometimes, you know when the phone is about to ring or who is calling before you pick it up.

I am often intuitive—I will mention, out of the blue, someone I've not seen for months or even years and, uncannily, within a short while, that person phones. Most of us can remember these common examples of intuition at work. One successful stockbroker accounted for his judgment calls, saying, "I just have these feelings to buy a certain stock. Even though I cannot always back it up with logical analysis, I try to still my skeptical mind and follow my hunches. It usually works out."

A manager I worked with is in charge of hiring people for her department. She says, "I just know within myself if they are going to work or not, even if their experience implies something different." She has an enviable track record with her hiring so far.

The point is, as with the other forms of intelligence and skill development, most people can learn proficiency when they focus on sharpening that function. Most of us can learn to play and enjoy music, write poetry, become computer engineers or guidance counselors, play tennis, and so on. So, too, we can learn to develop our subtle faculties of innate intuitive intelligence.

> *Granting yourself regular "training" time*
> *allows your intuitive intelligence to develop,*
> *making you more consciously available and accessible.*

A Growth of Spirit

You can expect to feel a growth of spirit, a union or connection with others, a special kinship, when you are in a deeper relationship with your inner world. Your attitude becomes kinder and more generous, not just toward others but also toward yourself. You may feel more compassion toward others, not criticizing so quickly or rushing to conclusions. You may perceive larger, more interconnected patterns. You may feel and extend increased genuine goodwill towards others. You may notice a feeling of being less pressured to please others out of guilt or personal deficit. You may adopt a learning attitude to many of life's stresses.

As you focus inwardly day after day, you are less likely to condemn and more likely to embrace others with decreased judgment. As they gain a sense of their inner selves, most people begin to integrate a larger, more global view, finding it easier to reach out in mutual respect to others.

John told of his newfound generosity of spirit after he started sitting quietly with his eyes closed for ten minutes every morning. He worked in a garage as a mechanic and was always critical of his co-workers and customers.

"I used to feel self-righteous because I thought all these guys were dumb. They would ask me what I thought were dumb questions, and the customers were even worse. I would complain and talk bad about them behind their backs. Then I got sick with some stomach thing, which scared me.

"My doctor told me I needed to relax and learn how to handle my stress better. He told me to meditate for ten minutes every morning before I went to work and gave me this tape to follow. I was so scared of losing my job that I started to do it even though I thought it was pretty weird. I'd sit down before work and listen to a talking tape about relaxing and thinking good thoughts.

"It made me think about myself. I began to see after a little while that I was becoming a nicer guy. I mean, I wasn't so quick to judge others who I thought were so dumb all the time. My head wasn't filled with angry thoughts all the time. I began to slow down and be more patient with people. Seems funny to me, but I kind of like it now. I am not always so tied up in knots thinking others are dumb—and my stomach is better, too."

Self-Respect

Your enhanced ability to respect yourself, entering into a meaningful and constructive relationship with your needs, also extends to others. This may mean that certain long-standing personal relationships are replaced with new, more empowering ones. Renewed self-respect often comes with new boundaries where, perhaps before, there were none. You'll no longer tolerate abusive, demeaning, demanding, or disrespectful treatment, even from old friends and family members. Behaviors you may have uncomfortably tolerated in the past are no longer acceptable.

A new sense of self moves you away from being a victim. At the same time, you become more tolerant of other behaviors—your own and others'—that may have been annoying in the past. You become more accepting of personality quirks. You see that everyone is on their own path, and while some may harmonize with your life purposes, others are better left on their own.

Both responses clarify your values: what you find disrespectful and just idiosyncratic. The more you respect and care for yourself, the more you can create mutually empowering relationships while allowing other relationships to drop away. This becomes an upward-expanding spiral.

The respect and understanding you feel for yourself and others
fuels your success in work, play, and every area of life.

Dick demonstrates a feeling that is not unusual. When he shared that he had trouble opening up to people and felt criticized by others, no one in the group doubted him for a minute. He sat in an utterly closed posture—arms and legs crossed, chin on chest, eyes glued to the floor. Yet it was evident that he desperately wanted to have friends.

During our workshop, he learned to focus inward and identify what he wanted and did not want. He then did mind lifts. He visualized himself as being more relaxed and open. He began to mentally experience himself laughing with others, becoming aware of his strengths. He imagined speaking up to those who criticized him, cutting short any disrespect for himself. He would affirm feeling more relaxed and open by saying, "I feel good about this. I can relax."

Dick opened up, gradually feeling safe enough to extend himself to the other people in the group and also letting in their support and affection. He began to trust himself more. It didn't happen overnight, but Dick made some necessary first steps in his discovery of respecting himself.

The last time I saw him, he said, "I continue to amaze myself. I am more open with people and increasingly laugh and enjoy myself. Other people don't walk over me anymore."

His self-esteem and confidence continue to increase with each success, and, in his way, he is increasingly a hero to himself. "Ultimately, I am the only one who determines if I am successful and okay. I'm feeling more in charge."

> *The purpose of inner mind work is to learn*
> *how to expand and nurture yourself creatively.*

As children, most of us did not learn how to practice thinking the best of ourselves. Children are raised to behave and may be told not to be arrogant or "full of themselves." You may have a vague idea about self-respect or self-love, but for many people, it is hard to look in the mirror and easily say the words "I love you." Reasonable mental and emotional health means honoring your own inner strength and awareness. It is essential work. Acknowledgment is an integral part of maximizing potential and creativity. Very simply, a daily time of reflection and inner focusing helps you learn to approach the world not from the "half-empty glass" viewpoint but from the generosity of spirit of an empowered person.

> *Self-love is an acquired skill.*
> *It grows through nurturing and practice.*

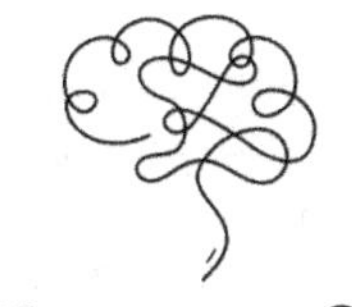

Chapter 22

A Life Artist

"Life is not about 'or' — it is about 'and.'"
~Kristin Nelson

CREATING YOUR LIFE attitudes is a high-energy, invigorating venture. You become an artist in life, absorbed in the moment-to-moment experience. Time expands. Stress is replaced with increased appreciation and a sense of grace. Not always, but increasingly. There is flow, an absorption leaving "no ordinary moments," as Dan Millman writes in *The Way of the Peaceful Warrior*. You become increasingly aware of an invisible balance between creating and surrendering to the momentary reality.

In his funny and imaginative book *Skinny Legs and All*, Tom Robbins says, "Those people who recognize that imagination is reality's master, we call 'sages,' and those who act upon it we call 'artists.'" Artists capture life experience and give it form. Sages sense life as something more significant and wholly interconnected. You can become both.

You may feel yourself become, at the same time, a creator, listener, and observer of the process of living, with a feeling of wonder at its mysteries. Your observing self may feel like a butterfly riding softly on your shoulder. It is a true paradox that purposefully creating and trusting the intuitive must be held in the same breath. Thinking of yourself as a life artist encourages you to experience the balancing and changing nature of daily living, with its simplicities and intricacies. You become more watchful and less judgmental of how you fit into the whole. You then see an artistic expression in everything because you bring a quality of integrity and excellence to everything you do.

The life artist develops a listening, contemplative outlook.
This imagination and authenticity affect the day-to-day way you live. You experience a new sense of fullness resulting from the quality and character of self-choices in your life. You know that direction and courage will be there when you need them to show the way. You feel an unexplained trust that moment by moment, you will be able to respond fully in the very best way possible for you.

Some Empowered Attitudes

Keep reminding yourself of where you want to be going. The list keeps growing as you move from stress and constraint to health and openness.

- Your initial reactions to new people and things are welcoming and optimistic. You are open to the possibility that events and things may be forces for the good in your life.
- You value a sense of humor. You laugh at yourself and easily have fun.
- You are open and share yourself with others, moving away, if necessary, from those who disrespect or abuse you in any way.
- You are aware of your self-limits and fears, knowing that they represent only a part of your experience, not all of it.
- You do not have to worry about whether or not you are content and even happy—because you are.
- You do what feels right for you because you trust your intuition.
- You meet each day with self-confidence and realistic, optimistic expectations rather than a gnawing dread or depression.
- You have compassion and respect for yourself and others. You give freely without feeling that you are making a sacrifice. You want to be supportive of the best in each person. You can admire others because you do not fear that if they win, you lose.
- You feel worthy, empowered, and sufficiently controlled to handle the tasks before you.
- You let ideas of who you are and what you want to do emerge from within yourself rather than having them dictated by external forces.

- You are gently self-disciplined. You are focused and have clear priorities.
- You feel a harmonious balance among many aspects of your life.

Creative Thinking Exercise

1. Close your eyes and relax. Pause a while, just being with your breath. Consciously call on your imaging talents to stimulate your imagination. As a life artist, start with silly things such as all ordinary people walking on their hands instead of their feet—anything that springs to mind—and play with the images freely. Or, you can imagine a situation at work that would be entirely off the wall, such as having a banquet, complete with a live band for management and staff, for every Friday's lunch.

2. Change your imagination exercise to focus on moments when you felt the generosity of someone reaching out to you with a feeling of friendship and understanding. Visually recall such a time. Focus on your feelings, thoughts, and attitude. In what ways can you imagine yourself reaching out to someone—a coworker, a neighbor, a family member, or someone in the community?

3. Pick one or two times you have recently taken care of yourself. Anything—big or small—will do. Think quietly about precisely what you did to care for yourself gently and kindly. Allow your mind to think of the different possibilities self-care engenders.

To gather fuel for this exercise, carry around the idea of creative thinking and notice when you experience an example of creativity, a flash of intuitive knowing, and a moment of dynamic love in your daily life. Be aware of a new insight, a hint of a problem solved, a good feeling with another, and even a glimmer of how the future might develop for you. Please take note of these moments, writing them down so you can grow familiar with your personal pattern of life artistry.

Chapter 23

Getting Ready

Mind Fitness is to the mind what physical fitness is to the body.

In Chapter Six, we did a quick Mind Fitness booster. Now, let's look first at prepping for your fuller mental fitness session.

Whatever the length, a Mind Fitness inner mind workout has the same three main parts: you want to focus on your breath to enter a state of aware relaxation, followed by visualizing and affirming an intention.

Quick stretching warm-ups at the beginning and a self-reflective acknowledgment at the end add to the "workout." Remember that there is no right or wrong way to practice Mind Fitness. The only wrong way is not to allow yourself the time and space to pause and go inward for a few minutes daily. Everyone's program content will be personalized to fit their circumstances, personality traits, and life goals.

Twenty Minutes—More or Less

You can time yourself by setting an alarm clock or timer or letting the session end naturally. The goal is to work your way up to a comfortable ten to fifteen to twenty minutes a day spent in proactive reflection. About twenty minutes is the right amount of time for most people to spend on their daily Mind Fitness workout. Any less, and it isn't easy to get fully engaged and warmed up. Any more, and your attention may begin to wander.

As in physical fitness, a twenty-minute daily workout is good health maintenance. More may be better, but optional. One successful financial businessman told me that "the last four minutes were the best," the most peaceful, for him, so he set his alarm for twenty minutes and hit the four-minute snooze button when it rang.

The point is to stay sensitive to your rhythm. Judge for yourself how much time you need and want to take. Eventually, you may work up to a considerably longer time when your schedule allows. As you relax into the quiet, Mind Fitness becomes one of the most enjoyable parts of your day. It's easy, relaxing, and rejuvenating.

Mind Fitness is the "no-sweat way to sanity"!

As you encourage yourself to move into a regular inner-focusing time daily—or at least several times weekly, the idea is *not* to make yourself feel guilty because you miss a day or only manage five minutes in one day.

This is not a new weapon to beat yourself up with; it's a mental health program to help you live your daily life with less stress.

It's a mindful, mental fitness strategy, so give it a chance to work. The ideal for beginners is to get serious enough about yourself to commit to your inner workout a few days a week. I tell myself that I am doing fine if I do my Mind Fitness five out of seven days for ten to twenty minutes each time. Set a realistic goal for your busy life, and then hold on. That way, it becomes a part of your "real" daily life, not something extra and separate. Remember, you want to make this orientation in your thinking a *part* of you, as integrated into your life as other preventative health strategies: taking a shower, taking vitamins, or washing your hands. Doing it with others is a great support. I now do a 20-minute meditation on Zoom with people at a certain time. It keeps me engaged and offers structure to my practice.

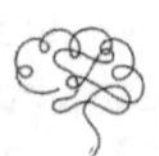

Physical to Mental: Stretching

Before you try to sit down and hold very still, take a minute or so to do some basic stretching. You can use any stretches you like. I've described some standard stretches to help you start, but please feel free to do others. Notice that I have included a mini-visualization and words of affirmation for each stretch. The body and mind are connected, so prepare both for your Mind Fitness practice as you visualize and affirm with each exercise.

Overhead stretch

Reach up high and do an overhead stretch. If you can, try to stand on your tiptoes as you reach. If you are sitting down, reach overhead with your arms and stretch from the rib cage. Visualize yourself growing and extending as you reach for a ball stuck in a tree. Visualize the ball as the goal you'll focus on in your session, and reach high. Stretch the highest you can as you exhale all the air in your lungs. Say to yourself: *I can reach any goal I set my mind on.*

Corkscrew swing

This exercise releases the spine with a twist or horizontal swinging motion. Stand with your feet about shoulder-width apart and turn from side to side, allowing your arms to swing out. You can also do this seated; rotate from the waist. Try to see behind yourself as you twist from side to side, allowing your spine to release. Turn your head with your body, watching your hands as they swing. Swing from side to side several times, exhaling through your mouth with some force or gush of air. As you are swinging, with quick little exhales, visualize yourself as flexible rubber band, and perhaps say to yourself: *I am flexible and adaptable.*

Shoulder rolls

These are great for releasing mental and physical burdens and duties—tension immediately drains away as you release your shoulders. You can stand or sit for this one. Try raising your shoulders toward your ears and then, after holding for a moment, rotate them to the back and down in a circular motion. You can do this any time—at your desk, driving, waiting in line—to release tension in your shoulders and neck. Again, exhale as you do this and feel the tensions drop off. Visualize yourself jumping on a trampoline and affirm: *I am loose and ready for success.* Try doing five shoulder rolls for a good release.

Turtleneck stretch

The Turtleneck stretch helps relax the nervous system and promote calmness. It's a favorite to do in the car or at your desk. As you breathe in, lower your chin as if trying to touch your chest. You will feel a good stretch of the spine. Hold for a moment. Slowly exhale, raising your chin to a level position while squeezing your shoulders toward your ears again, as you did in the second exercise. Hold and then release your shoulders to their normal position. Feel a flood of tension leaving your body.

You can do the turtleneck stretch just sitting in a chair whenever you want to pause and breathe. Visualize a turtle or a crane raising and lowering its head as you affirm: *I calm myself and release nervous tension.*

Finger lace stretch

Standing or sitting, place your palms together, interlacing your fingers, then turn them outward and extend your arms as far as they will go. Push out as you curve your chest inward, stretching your back muscles. Exhale as if you were about to whistle a good tune. Visualize love and good health, filling the circle your arms have made, and affirm: *I embrace good health.* Straighten your back, bringing your hands back to your chest, turning your palms inward, back to your palms touching.

Filling an invisible ball

Stand or sit with your feet shoulder-width apart. Slowly and with great attention, bring your hands over your head as you stretch up to the sky, inhaling fully. Slowly, while releasing your breath in a steady stream, lower your arms with your hands in front of you, palms up, until your hands are at waist level, about three inches apart. Visualize yourself holding an invisible ball of energy. Affirm to yourself: *I am filling myself with positive energy that fuels my thinking.*

Getting Comfortable

Preparation means positioning yourself to be comfortable without interruptions. Ideally, do your inner mind workout in the same place and at the same time each day. That is ideal, but it may only be practical for some people, so sit down anywhere you can on a cushion, at your desk, or in the bathtub. You can do your session while riding in a carpool, train, or bus. You can lie down, but the trick is to not go to sleep. Sitting up is the preferred posture to be relaxed yet calmly alert.

I prefer two positions. One is sitting cross-legged with a small cushion under me. Placing my hands and feet in the same position each practice session allows me to reach my still center more quickly. It is as if that posture clues my mind to relax and let go.

The second position is sitting in a chair with my feet flat on the floor, my back straight, and my head easily balanced on my neck. This works well in airports, waiting rooms, or office situations.

***Explore different meditation techniques and postures
to determine which is best for you.***

A familiar posture makes reaching and maintaining a state of relaxation easier as your body and mind pick up the cue. My cue to myself is to touch my fingertips together, which helps me move more quickly to a sense of calmness and on to inner seeing and directed words. Over time, your body position builds up its own suggestive power. Whatever your posture and place, whether alone or in groups, please take a few moments to make it yours and settle in. Tell yourself that this is your time to mindfully stop, empty out, take stock of your day, and prepare for future actions with direction.

Proactive reflection involves stopping, looking, and listening.

You may want to read or listen to inspirational materials. Preparing yourself helps you open to another way of viewing your life and the world. Doing this helps me relax and go to a deeper, more meaningful inner place.

***Mind Fitness is a deep-centered approach that regularly encourages
a conscious focus on your body, mind, and spirit.***

Chapter 24

Three Steps to Your Mind Fitness "Workout"

"Wherever you are is the entry point."
~**Kabir**

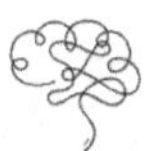

Step 1: Focused Relaxation—Unifying Mind and Body

The key to aware relaxation is to take a breather. Literally. Your breath is the key. Make it steady and smooth. Breathe full, deep breaths into your abdominal area. Focus on your breathing, and consciously feel the breath entering and leaving your body. Counting each inhalation and exhalation is mind-focusing. Invite a sense of quietness to come over you. You can use your mind's eye to scan down your body, consciously releasing tension. Shoulders, fingers, and toes often hold tension. Tell yourself that you are giving yourself permission to completely relax your body and mind for the next few minutes. With practice, you can enjoy the experience of what it feels like to be entirely at peace with yourself for just a few moments.

You can sing, hum, or repeat a few words to focus your thinking while breathing quietly. A mantra is simply repeating words that allow your mind to still its random chatter. I like the simple repetition of "Peace" for myself. As you become familiar with how your personal physical and mental relaxation feels, it will be easier to maintain it at other times during your day. You are teaching yourself something new—a skill that can be used in many situations.

Buddhist monk and author Thich Nhat Hanh recommends a simple practice to center yourself and gain deeper awareness. As you inhale, say, "Calming body and mind." As you exhale, smile slightly.

On the second inhalation, say "Present moment," and with the exhalation, "Only moment." So it goes:

"Calming body and mind—

[Half smile]—

Present moment—

Only moment."

I enjoy this meditation practice a great deal. I don't think Thich Nhat Hanh would mind me passing it along to you. He has written many books, and I heartily recommend looking for them. They are simple to read, wise, and heartfelt, with a poetic rhythm to his writing.

Invite the Intuitive

Relaxation occurs naturally as you experience your breath flowing in and out, in and out, easing tension and pausing action in both body and mind, allowing your intuitive intelligence to be accessed.

After consciously releasing your muscular tensions with the breath, you can focus on opening to your intuition. Open yourself to images and flashes of intuitive insight and wisdom that may come unexpectedly on random subjects.

Intuition does not shout; its soft voice needs quiet to coax it out. A new idea or thought may come to you during or after your practice. Stay aware of synchronicities and new flashings of insight. You are developing intuitive intelligence by allowing it time and attention, and the fruits of your mindful awareness may pop up at any time. If nothing comes to you, relax and enjoy the quiet time, feeling no pressure. Put aside the thoughts "I should be doing…" or "I ought to be more..." You are doing precisely what is best for your overall health and well-being. Relax and quietly center within your body and mind. If you need a "should," you can remember that you are doing exactly what research is reporting you *should* be doing, so resist the temptation to judge yourself with prearranged action-oriented expectations.

Think of this as a doctor-prescribed mini-vacation.
You can mentally travel anywhere, and anything can happen.

Step 2: Visual Thinking—Giving Yourself a Road Map

Visual thinking means seeing clear pictures within your mind's eye. Like a zoom lens, your mind can focus close up or take in a wide-angle view. The close-up view is analytical, looking at things from all angles, while the contextual view is more like telling yourself a story. Be aware of what you are visualizing. We don't want to visualize anger and fears but to concentrate on visualizing goals and ideals rather than getting caught up in dead-end loops of anxieties.

Again, remember, you are opening to your intuitive sense—allow its whisperings and hunches to guide your thinking. If you aim to be more patient with a family member, create little scenes in your mind in which you play that more patient role, picturing your small actions and the overall feeling of patience. Focus on the most ideal, the most forgiving scene you can imagine. If you aim toward a tangible goal, such as purchasing a house, take the time to picture yourself attaining your home by visualizing the steps needed to get you there. Proactively work your imagination to see constructive pictures and images.

If you try to focus on too many things, your energy will get scattered,
and your visual thinking will need to be clearer and more effective.

Remember, when you expand one aspect of your beliefs, you affect all of yourself. You are planting a seed for future, more integrated attitudes and actions.

- See, feel, and experience yourself getting out of bed in the morning with the attitude you want to carry during the day.
- See, feel, and experience yourself moving through your day, taking care of your daily tasks with a new lightness and a sense of humor.
- See yourself handling a situation as you want to handle it.
- See, feel, hear, and experience yourself responding to someone who has been a problem.

Give yourself a road map of how you would ideally feel and act, then detach from the results and allow the process to occur.

If any roadblocks or cynicism slip into your visual thinking, stop, acknowledge the roadblock, and then mentally change what needs to be changed. Experience a sense of self-appreciation for taking the time and effort to release yourself from limiting attitudes and to learn new, more self-validating ways of thought and action. Allow your intuitive intelligence to guide you in your self-education.

The key is to fill your visual images with details and feelings. Make them come alive. Be outrageous! Make them as vivid and as accurate as you possibly can. Imagine the context, the actions, and the personal characteristics that would best help you develop your life goals and relationships.

You can become what you imagine. Make an impression on yourself.

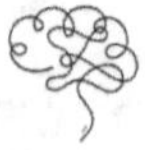

Step 3: Directed Word Power—Articulating/ Affirming

Put into words your stated intention and your direction of choice. You can choose to affirm, then visualize, or to visualize, then affirm. The order is not particularly important, but the combination of visual and auditory language is.

Precise words carry great power within our conscious minds, so use them with care and focus. And yes, affirmations will sound idealistic and even silly at times. Don't let that stop you. They are statements of your goals and ideals as if everything were attainable and possible. Use these general affirming thoughts and ask yourself how you feel about them being true.

- I am an insightful person who can handle whatever problems may arise.
- I am gifted with the ability to listen and communicate clearly.
- People sense my competency and want me to work with them.
- I trust I will know what I must do at the right moment.
- I am optimistic about my life and relationships.
- I look forward to seeing the humor in different circumstances.
- I am so grateful to be grateful.

That last affirmation came to me one day, just popping into my head. It is now one that I find myself using a lot of the time. You'll find that words come first from your familiar intellect and then may be followed by a more powerful, intuitive phrase. That is what happened to me. Be bold. Be inventive. What is your ideal? Try several different phrases until you feel or sense the one that is right for the moment.

***These short, directive phrases help keep your mind
focused on your conscious intentions.***

You aim to replace long-standing mental habits of internally hearing negative and fearful messages. You want to keep uncovering these undermining doubts. Forgive yourself for these doubts, then repeat your chosen words with feeling a few times to get your mind going in your new direction. Yes, it is like a mental game you are playing with yourself. You are in training to move forward, not backward.

At first, these clear sentences of idealized direction will feel strange. Expect that; say them anyway. Refrain from doubt that your intentions can be actualized as you constructively focus your mind and emotions.

In time, these affirming thoughts will begin to replace downers and come naturally to you.

Close with Self-Reflection and Acknowledgment

At the close of your Mind Fitness session, consider reflecting on your inner experience and making a few notes in your mind or a journal.

- Did a meaningful phrase come to you?
- Can you recall and label your sensations and feelings?
- How easy was it for you to feel relaxed in your body and mind?
- What have you noticed about your personal rhythm and energy cycles?

Writing for a few minutes at the end of your session is a powerful way to track your inner mind changes. New attitudes are like infants: unsteady and fragile. You need to nourish and build attitudes up to be solid and self-determined. You want your new perspective and attitudes to be automatic, not afterthoughts. That is the transition you aim to make; it comes with perseverance.

Keep yourself focused on the person you want to be
rather than letting outside circumstances
dictate your attitude and inner dialogue.

A balanced mind does not happen only in these quiet times. The goal is to create a clear direction as part of your ongoing life, which will be present throughout the day. You may not always be in your perfect place or posture, but that does not mean you cannot direct yourself clearly and meaningfully toward a sense of inner peace and goal attainment.

Acknowledge yourself.
Most importantly, say thank you to yourself!

You took the time and intention to work on your mental health and sense of self. You allowed yourself to move from stress to increased calm, from non-awareness to awareness. Saying thank you to yourself affirms that you are doing things for your own well-being and sense of direction. Congratulations!

Resistance

You may feel awkward or uncomfortable the first few times you go through your routine, and you probably will. Most people do. Resistance occurs mainly as "This stuff will not help me. It is mind play and silliness." Resistance may come from unfamiliarity with the process and the fear of change—especially of changing yourself. Creating a new thinking pattern takes time. Just know that this feeling will lessen, and you will soon start to feel like you are living more in the moment. Creating rather than coping becomes exciting as you begin to feel the results.

Practicing each day consistently guides you from
old, destructive habits into new, life-affirming thinking patterns.

Being a life artist means creating more of the life you want with your values and sense of contentment and happiness resulting from your attitudes and actions.

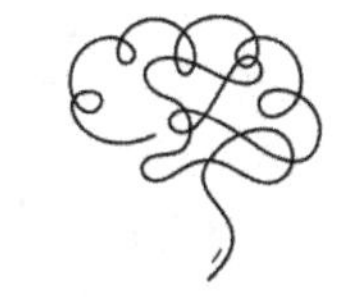

Chapter 25

A Stop and Relax Script

"The only time that is yours is the present."
~Grenville Kleiser

THE FOLLOWING PEACEFUL meditation assembles the sections previously presented. This script can also be found in the Mind Fitness book, *The Up Side of Being Down: Healing the Dis-Ease of Negativity with Mind Fitness*. It is most helpful in moving the body and mind into a state of solid relaxation. Reading through it a few times gives you a good sense of the feelings and self-talk to focus on. Remember that you are your own guide, so say it in a way that makes sense to you. Please read and record any of the scripts offered in this book. They will guide you into images for quiet relaxation and stimulate your own words for mental fitness.

I am taking the time to sit down and relax now because it is good for me. It brings me pleasure and peace of mind and is vital for my body. As I silence my mind, my breathing becomes deeper and fuller, my heart beats slower, and I can feel my muscles loosening, reaching a place of inner peace.

I am taking this reflection time daily to improve my health and well-being and welcome new thoughts and feelings that benefit me. When my mind can rest quietly, it also brings insight and creative ideas—in pictures, sensations, or words. This is when I can fill my mind with thoughts of fullness, of my dreams for myself and the world.

As I take a deep breath, I feel the flood of quietness reaches every part of my body. I imagine a golden, honey-colored light pouring down through the top of my head. I feel the release as the light touches my eyes, melting all the tension in my cheeks and through my mouth, throat, and neck, inviting me to give in to its warmth and release the tightness in my shoulders, arms, wrists, and fingertips.

I draw another deep and full breath, shifting the breathing from my chest to my ribs and lower abdomen. I breathe in again deeply, expanding my rib cage as I hold the air in my lower abdomen for a moment and slowly let it out through my lips. I feel the richness of the moment alive within me. I allow the quieting to move through my chest, back, stomach, and lower intestines, then down through my groin, legs, and feet, relaxing and letting go of all tension.

As I take another full breath, I feel the increased oxygen circulating through my body and brain. I call on the power of my concentrated mind to focus on one thing and hold that point. I will focus on an image of a peaceful pond with a big shade tree on its shore, with cattails and other reeds growing around it. The pond is serene. There are no ripples on its surface. It is entirely tranquil. I inhale a sweet scent, filling my mind with images of this pond. I let go of any other thoughts I may have, focusing on the tranquility of my mind and emotions and the relaxation of my body.

I know that as I focus on the pond and its stillness, my mind will stop whirling around and come to rest. After my relaxation and peace, I can more easily accomplish all my needs.

I take in another deep breath and let go of any tensions my body may still be holding as I reflect once again on the pond and its quietness—the beauty of the water's reflection, the fullness of the green tree, and the gentleness of the reeds as they grow near the water's edge.

The image of my relaxed body is that of a sleeping cat, totally at peace with the world, purring in its most contented way, with not a tight muscle anywhere. My body becomes like a cat's—loose, limp, totally at one with the world around me. My body feels heavy as I release any nervous energy.

From this still place within my mind and body,
I can feel the intuitive sense beginning to form my awareness.
I feel that presence of wholeness, of beauty, of total tranquility. I feel that bubble of spirit rise, giving new meaning to something I had been worried about during the day. This clear bubble that I imagine is a spiritual essence within me that unifies my body, mind, and heart.

I ask in this state of quietness for guidance about how to live my life, solve my problems, and best contribute.

(Your intuition may offer new ideas and thoughts. It is not mysterious; you get an idea, a thought, or a feeling.)

I take another deep breath, knowing that I have taken time to nourish myself and connect my body and spirit. I know that this inner time helps my body heal, allowing my mind and emotions reach a point of clarity, and my heart to touch a gentle healing place.

I feel myself awakening to the reality around me. I begin to wiggle my fingers and toes, take a deep breath, slowly open my eyes, and feel refreshed and unified in body, mind, and heart, knowing that I did something good for myself today.

Review: A Mind Fitness "Workout"

Do a complete inner mind routine, the "No Sweat Way!"

- Stretch to warm up and release muscle tension.
- Prepare yourself and your posture to be peaceful and comfortable.
- Breathe and relax as you quiet your mind and body.
- Open to your intuitive sense by focusing on being open, peaceful, and relaxed.
- Visualize your goal as you would ideally have it occur.

- Articulate your intention. Affirm your ideally stated goal.
- Close with a clear and reflective mindset.
- Acknowledge yourself for taking the time to do something beneficial for yourself mentally and spiritually.

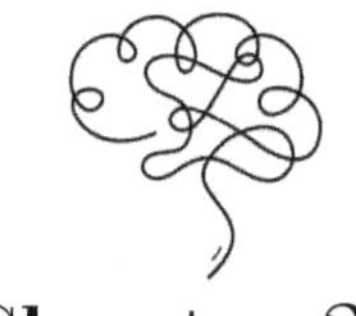

Chapter 26

Personal Change Ripples Out

"Our most urgent and pressing need is to provide that wonderful instrument… the human mind with the wherewithal to image and thereby create a better world."
~Jonas Salk

PEOPLE WITH EMPOWERED mental fitness can respond to life's challenges using intuitive and critical thinking skills, calling upon inner guidance and outer questioning. This kind of thinking encompasses the whole and the sequences of its parts. This power of thought supports individuals in walking their path through life with a balanced optimism and inner connection. We cannot give this power to another person, but we can cultivate its growth within ourselves and encourage it within those we touch.

As the inner self awakens, the outer self responds with growing calmness with yourself and others. Inner fitness develops mental clarity and spiritual insight. A sense of peace replaces stress. You respond to outer stimulation more often with trust rather than reacting with panic. You replace that trapped feeling with a choice of empowerment. You act upon inner responsibility and guidance. As our individual character is built paradoxically, definitions of separation are softened. Personal and social needs, creativity, and intuitive thinking join together. From this profound inner union, personal, emotional, and social peace are learned, and sage and artist stand side by side.

> ***The time spent within your silence allows you to***
> ***develop your unique patina and texture of character.***
> ***It becomes your soul walk.***

Group Relationships Are Strengthened

One way to experience union is by joining with others to spend time in silence or socializing while walking, especially in nature, sitting, and eating together. This fosters a sense of well-being and direction. Both the quiet and socializing carry within it the seeds of union and relationship. A rich new dimension develops. The physical routine can be open, allowing people to follow their rhythms while at the same time offering a structure of activities.

Retreat days or half days, in which you seek out time and space to reflect, reward you with a new awareness of and union with yourself. Oddly enough, one visible result you will notice is that you are more outgoing and available when you are with people. A retreat time does not make you want to go off and be a hermit full-time. Instead, it is more like filling your gas tank: you have much more to offer to yourself and others.

This state of interrelationship is a spiritual mindset and attitude that crosses all activities. It is a feeling of balanced mental health, a sense of calm you can experience not only on retreat days but during any focused activity: hiking, doing crossword puzzles or Sudoku, dancing, bicycling, cooking, model building, or bird watching. Some people take up an art form, visual, musical, or language. Some sit quietly admiring the beauty. The ways to experience union within yourself are as varied as individual people.

What's essential for empowered mental well-being is to experience your own version of peace, consciously and with intention. As you open to the meditation and the rhythms found in your life experiences, the judgments you were so sure of in the past begin to soften. You feel the interrelationship and union as an attitude, a way of living that moves from yourself to others.

***Any time you do something that brings
you deep joy, you are in a place of union.***

Nothing is more demanding of calmness, creativity, and union than working and living in close relationships. Here, you will witness some powerful pulls. As personal and social development become desirable goals, some of the more common dysfunctional behavior experienced in family and work groups begins to lessen. A group can be any two or more individuals who come together in a relationship: housemates, department workers, a school class, a playing team, or a family unit.

A group oriented toward learning handles the inevitability of constant change differently than a group trying to keep everything the same. When change is accepted as part of the desired process rather than seen as something to be avoided at all costs, the whole tone of the group relationship becomes more supportive. It becomes expected and accepted for people to make mistakes, to grow and develop, pushing past their comfort zones into new areas of interaction and self-awareness. The group norm is that they do not have to be perfect experts to garner respect or even act like they did yesterday or last month. The slogan "Catch 'em being good!" speaks to this affirmation. Constructive change in both attitudes and actions is permitted and encouraged.

I asked a group of children, "What are you most proud of about yourself?" Vic, a ten-year-old with a history of school problems, answered, "I am changing and growing, and I like that about myself. I am becoming a good student now." Vic had gained a definition, a purpose, an affirmation he could understand, and a support group to help him reach his goal.

When change and growth are accepted, we are less likely to resort to hidden teasing and verbal sabotaging. Instead of such words and actions, which undermine self-esteem and respect, we offer the support of acknowledgment: "I knew you could do it. Congratulations!"

With the emphasis on positive affirmation, kids, partners, and employees become less critical or blaming. Fundamental behavioral changes start. There is more kindness, more patience, and more support. We communicate and respect each other's boundaries and idiosyncrasies. We begin to honor each other.

With tears of joy, one woman told me that her whole department took up a financial offering to help support her brother's family after a serious car accident. "It means a lot to feel that kind of help now. It means we are not alone. I never knew this kind of love before." That is dynamic love in action…an office collection at the right moment.

Competition Expands to Collaboration

All groups respond to a change in attitude, however slowly. There's a shift from judgment to more open listening and acceptance. Action-oriented, dynamic love becomes visible while unhealthy competition and sarcastic backbiting fade away. The home, school, or office becomes a more actively supportive environment. Blaming and sarcastic teasing begin to lessen and may disappear as personal and group relationships grow. As their communication increases, people become more willing to be vulnerable on an emotional level, increasingly trusting each other.

This kind of attitude adjustment can be seen even when only one group member decides to grow. No doubt the lead person needs extra courage; it can feel risky being the first to foster a change in the general attitude climate. As you focus on your attitude and reactions, you will also see changes growing within your group. You will begin to see new ways of interacting with each other. It is also realistic and vital to remember that, like personal change, group change occurs at its own rate.

It takes persistence and belief in your power to expand and change.

Support Groups

Robert Muller, assistant secretary general to the United Nations for forty years and an extraordinary humanitarian and global thinker, wrote in his inspiring book *New Genesis*:

> *"Generation after generation will have to be educated in*
> *peace and global living if peace is to become*
> *a permanent feature on this planet."*

I was once invited to a meeting in Soviet Moscow, where medical, military, and scientific professionals presented their research findings regarding the human illness resulting from the nuclear accident at Chernobyl.

The number of stillbirths, cancers, and other malformations was staggering. Human suffering, unrelieved despite the present state of medical knowledge, would not go away with any amount of mental work.

When I was asked to speak on the application of Mind Fitness to this tragic situation, I felt overwhelmed. This was no mental tragedy; nuclear contamination is a physical reality. Finding my voice, I was grateful to speak from intuition on the one thing that can always help, no matter how desperate the situation—people connecting with care and understanding, both in life and when facing death: human relationship, contact, and compassion for each other. For my few minutes, I could portray the importance of fostering support groups to share personal comfort and courage.

Supporting each other with love and dignity is sometimes the best we can do for each other.

Sometimes, coping gracefully is the best you can do in a difficult situation. There can be power in joining together to share and comfort each other. This lifts some of the helplessness and restores basic human dignity.

Support groups may not physically resolve the situation, but they do give us an avenue to regain some control over our reactions. Within a group, there are always times when some feel stronger than others. The group sharing of understanding can make all the difference in the world. Just knowing you are not alone but are connected and in a relationship with others provides a sense of courage and self-determination. It's a paradox: the giver is also the receiver. When you give love, the true gift freely returns to you.

We can find power and healing in a group dedicated to simply listening and being present with each other. Such sharing of vulnerabilities inspires intimacy and engenders positive mental health and emotional care. Groups carry many names: study groups, religious groups, dream groups, recovery groups, women's and men's groups, couples' groups, church-affiliated groups, and healing groups. Even corporate focus and task groups can have such personal elements.

Listening to others expands your frame of reference. This joining and sharing create a vulnerability and intimacy that fuels health, performance, and overall well-being. I encourage you to set up a private discovery group for a couple of months to do the exercises in this book. You will find it an enriching experience.

Think in Ideals

As you experiment with quiet awareness training and proactive thinking, you will find that the results are worth your time and focus. You create and manifest expanded possibilities. Energy follows thought. Matter follows intention. Unbalance grows into balance. Stress to Sanity becomes a reality. You are now aiming in your desired direction, following your highest and best intentions. This is not striving for perfection but for a calm assurance. Yes, as with physical fitness, it takes time and effort, but you will find the results worth your time and focus. Committing to consciously developing yourself to your full potential is to take action on your soul's urging. Limitations begin to melt away, and a source of strength grows in the face of self-doubt. Confidence in your abilities leads to a life path of compassion and dynamic love.

I am serene and peaceful.

Appendix: Images of Health Script

This is a daily time of self-care and tranquility.
This is the time to form images of health for yourself.

To stay healthy, you must recognize the need to take quiet, intimate time just for yourself. This healing meditation script is designed to help you slow down and embrace the more inward and gentler pace needed to stay healthy and balanced.

"Images of Health" fosters an attitudinal approach. It empowers your body, mind, and heart to awaken the intellectual potential and love within yourself. By taking a few moments to relax each day, you train yourself to quiet your body and mind in what grows to be a very meaningful and deep communion, promoting personal health and well-being. The program combines physical awareness with Mind Fitness. It will guide you to activate your mind through imagery and affirmation as you learn how to relax. This body, mind, and heart approach encourages you to become friends with your body to remain centered and in control, promoting personal healing and best performance.

You can record this for yourself. You will find it very empowering.

Relaxation

Take a deep breath. // Feel the warmth of your breath flood through you, touching you from within. / With the exhalation, let everything go. ///

Feel your breath warming your skin, encouraging your muscles to relax, / your nerves to quiet as you release thoughts and deeply relax for a few moments in gentle peace with your body. /// That's right. You are doing a good job.

Let the warmth of your breath enter your head, / let your mouth soften, / let your tongue rest gently in your mouth as you feel your jaw and lips soften. //

Let your eyelids soften and rest quietly over your eyes as you take a full breath, encouraging your breath to bring quieting warmth to your neck and shoulders. ///

Release your shoulders and feel your upper back expand as your muscles become more and more relaxed. //

Breathe in, feeling the quieting warmth travel down your arms, // caressing the palms of your hands. // Let your breath flood out of each finger. ///

Take a full breath. // Let the warmth fill your lungs and heart. /// Let the breath fill your chest as your thoughts float away in the vast spaciousness of your mind. Breathe deeply into your torso, into your belly, and your hips. Let go of any tightness you may feel / and gently move the relaxation to your thighs, // your knees, and down your calves as the warmth floods out each toe. //

Now, once again, take a complete, peaceful breath. // Imagine your heart pulsing within you as your breath brings oxygen to your bloodstream, nourishing your entire body, every cell. //

Take a breath. /// Relax. // Invite the touch of your breath to massage every muscle and organ in your body. // Let your body and mind deeply rest in a deep, quiet peacefulness. //

Visualization

We promote health in ourselves when we let go of conflict and allow a sense of acceptance within ourselves. Illnesses can come to us sometimes because we are carrying the burden of feelings that are painful to us. We may have been carrying these unhappy feelings for many years.

In the quiet of your mind, I invite you to see yourself putting down the burdens of conflict and fear. These may be guilt for something you have done, anger toward someone you have carried, or disappointment that life turned out differently than you had hoped. One by one, lay those heavy feelings down in the grass as you forgive anything that needs to be forgiven, and feel your body relaxing as you let go. That's right. Just let them go.

Wherever you experience pain, let the image of the ocean wave carry you through it. Imagine the pain as a wave to ride. You don't want to be wiped out and pulled under. You want to ride it, staying on top and accepting its challenge. Image yourself atop the crest of the wave, relaxed and vital at the same time.

This is the time to form images of health for yourself. See yourself doing gratifying things. Remember times in your life when you felt healthy and vibrant. See the people you are with and places you like. Take the time now to be gentle and caring of yourself.

Imagine walking across a meadow or in the park on a warm, sunny day. It is spring, with yellow and red flowers and green grass. The sun feels warm on your back, and the breeze is soft in your hair. Feel how good it feels as you ask for and accept a new level of health and happiness for yourself. Whatever part of your body may need to be healed, see it bathed in a circle of warm sunlight. Feel it relax and feel better in the light. You are doing it just right.

Affirmations

With each breath, I fill my body with solid, robust health and vitality.

With each breath, I release my fears and focus my mind and heart on this moment of inner peace.

With each breath, I give others all the forgiveness I want others to give me. I can feel my body healing.

I can see all parts of my body working together, making me healthier every day.

With each breath, I bring loving care to my body as my body gives life to me. And with my new thinking, I bring loving care to our planet as our planet gives life to me.

I am now bringing light and warmth to each cell in my body. I can feel the healing occurring within me now.

I feel in control of my life as I focus my thoughts and love on giving as much as I can to others.

I invite you to remember when you felt healthy and fully alive. Imagine taking a walk on a sunny day, doing an art project, laughing, holding a child, or writing a poem; imagine anything pleasurable and meaningful to you. Please take a few moments to remember such a time and create it in your mind. As you remember a time you felt healthy and alive, see yourself as clearly as possible in your mind's eye and imagine experiencing that feeling again as wholly and entirely as you can. This is the healthy feeling you want to feel in your life right now.

Acknowledgements

I want to thank the many people who have allowed me into their lives. Their gifts of insight and love opened new horizons within me. In particular, I would like to thank John Widmer for the original cover design and the following people for their belief in and review of various stages of the initial work: Shirley Dockstader, Nancy Ringler, Hal Bennett, Jerry Jampolsky, Caron Goode, Deb Shanti, Thea Maestre, Carol Myers, Sue Lawson, William Miller, Karen Huguley, Monique Hanson, Ilene Kratka, Claire Boers-Stoll, Kale Lani Okazaki, Candi Harper, Patricia Stephens, Laura Sobol, Claire Russell, William Prescott, Kristi Hein, Betsy Hesser. Great appreciation, also, to editor Zora Knauf and publishing consultants Kristen Wise and Maira Pedierra of PRESStinely, who have supported this most recent edition of *From Stress to Sanity*.

Discussion Questions

I sincerely hope you found *From Stress to Sanity: It's About the Way You Think* a motivational read. In writing this book, I aimed to elevate your mental health to the same level of attention and concern as your physical fitness.

It is my hope that this book is read by individuals and is used by book groups, schools, and clinics as a learning model supporting mental health. The questions below were written to facilitate healthy conversations on various perspectives to enhance further understanding of the lessons learned.

Wishing you fruitful discussions,

Joy Watson

1. Exploring Inner Spaces: How does Joy L. Watson's concept of Mind Fitness expand your understanding of mental health beyond traditional approaches as described in *From Stress to Sanity*?
2. Carl Jung's Influence: How does the quotation from Carl Jung at the beginning of the book resonate with you in terms of the journey to reclaiming mental and physical health?
3. Practical Application: In what ways do the practical, evidence-based strategies outlined in *From Stress to Sanity* help you manage stress and cultivate mental clarity in your daily life?
4. Mind Fitness vs. Physical Fitness: Compare and contrast the principles of Mind Fitness introduced in the book with the concept of physical fitness. How do these parallels enhance your approach to overall wellbeing?
5. Love as Essence: Discuss the emphasis on love as the essence of being in Mind Fitness. How does this perspective influence the strategies and practices you find most impactful in *From Stress to Sanity*?

6. Personal Transformation: Share examples from the book where practical tools or strategies have led to personal transformation for you. How have these techniques contributed to changing your perceptions and behaviors?

7. From Stress to Sanity: What are the key takeaways from *From Stress to Sanity* that you believe can help you regain control and find peace amidst the chaos of modern life?

8. Empowerment and Attitudinal Healing: How does the concept of Attitudinal Healing, as discussed in the book, resonate with you? Discuss instances where changing attitudes has positively impacted your mental and physical health.

9. Reflection and Self-Directed Thinking: Reflect on the role of self-directed, reflective thinking in achieving mental clarity and emotional balance, as advocated in *From Stress to Sanity*.

10. Integration into Daily Life: How do you plan to integrate the principles and tools of Mind Fitness into your daily routines after reading *From Stress to Sanity*? Share your strategies and potential challenges in applying these concepts.

*Feel free to tailor these questions to your group's preferences and discussion style. Happy reading and discussing!

If your group is interested in a personal conversation with me, please contact me at www.mindfitness.com to discuss a virtual call.

I encourage you to share pictures of your group or your favorite reading spot with me. I also appreciate your book review on your retailer of preference.

Joy Watson
www.mindfitnessbooks.com
www.joywatson.com

About The Author

Joy Watson, M.Ed., has worked as an international communications and learning consultant. She has developed the integrated educational-health methodology known as Mind Fitness. Her work has been instrumental in maximizing human potential, personal and team success, and wellness. She has designed communication programs and has conducted seminars on Mind Fitness in business, education, and health. Joy, a human development educator with degrees in sociology and speech and language pathology from Boston University, is the author of several books on Mind Fitness, including *The Up Side of Being Down: Healing the Dis-Ease of Negativity with Mind Fitness, From Stress to Sanity: It's About the Way You Think,* and the latest book in the series, *Mind Fitness: A Guide to Elevating Mental Health.*